AN ALETHEA IN HEART PUBLICATION
IN THE SERIES OF

THE LIFE AND WORKS OF ASA MAHAN.

VOLUME II.

THE SYSTEM OF MENTAL PHILOSOPHY

REPUBLISHED BY THE EDITOR
RICHARD M. FRIEDRICH
ALETHEA IN HEART
8071 Main St.
Fenwick, MI 48834

(989) 637-4179

TruthInHeart.com

2005

THE ASA MAHAN PROJECT.

BY ALETHEA IN HEART MINISTRIES.
THE LIFE AND WORKS OF ASA MAHAN (1799-1889).

Volume

1. Doctrine of the Will. 1847.
2. The System of Mental Philosophy. 1882.
3. A System of Intellectual Philosophy. 1854.
4. The Science of Logic; or an Analysis of the Laws of Thought. 1857.
5. Science of Moral Philosophy. 1848.
6, 7. A Critical History of Philosophy in two Volumes. 1883.
8. The Science of Natural Theology. 1867.
9. Autobiography: Intellectual, Moral, and Spiritual. 1882.
10. The True Believer. 1847.
11. Scripture Doctrine of Christian Perfection. 1837, 1875.
12. Out of Darkness Into Light. 1877.
13. Baptism of the Holy Ghost. 1875.
14. Misunderstood Texts of Scripture. 1876.
15. Life Thoughts on the Rest of Faith. 1872.
16. Lectures on the Ninth of Romans. 1859.
17. The Phenomena of Spiritism; and, Spiritualism a Discussion. 1875.
18. Modern Mysteries Examined and Exposed. 1855.
19. A Critical History of the Late American War. 1877.
20. Miscellaneous Articles, Letters, and Index of the Complete Works.
    Physical and Moral Law Obligatory. 1839.
    The Relation of Christianity in the Freedom of Human Thought and Action. 1849.
    Dr. Mahan's Speech on the Crisis in the Protestant Episcopal Church in America. 1862.
    The Natural and the Supernatural in the Christian Life and Experience. 1878.
Numerous additional articles and literary notices in the following published periodicals:
    OE   The Oberlin Evangelist, 1839-1862
    OQR   The Oberlin Quarterly Review, 1845-1848
    BH   Banner of Holiness, 1872-1883
    DL   Divine Life and International Expositor of Scriptural Holiness, 1877-1889

Reproduction of the complete works in hard and soft covers is to be available in print individually and in a complete series. These works are available on CD, and will eventually have full searching capabilities. An audio recording of these works is also planned. Each sermon and lecture is to be made available as individual booklets. Mahan's contributions to *The Oberlin Evangelist*, *Oberlin Quarterly Review*, *Banner of Holiness*, and *Divine Life* are included in this.

Work books and multimedia helps are to be created to assist in the private or classroom study of these volumes. A presentation of the influence of Finney upon the church and world is to be given through the *American Reformation Project*.

THE

SYSTEM

OF

MENTAL PHILOSOPHY.

BY

ASA MAHAN, D.D., LL.D.

AUTHOR OF "THE SCIENCE OF INTELLECTUAL PHILOSOPHY,"
"THE SCIENCE OF LOGIC," "THE SCIENCE OF NATURAL THEOLOGY," ETC.

CHICAGO:

S. C. GRIGGS AND COMPANY,

1882.

Mahan, Asa, 1799-1889.
 The System of Mental Philosophy.
(The Life and Works of Asa Mahan Volume II.)

Republication of the 1882 ed. Published by S. C. Griggs, Chicago.

Library of Congress Control Number: 2005900115

ISBN 1-932370-67-6 Softcover edition.
ISBN 1-932370-44-7 (Volume II of *The Life and Works of Asa Mahan.*)

Second Alethea In Heart edition published in 2005.
Republished from the edition of 1882, Chicago, without altering anything but page numbers.

To order more copies visit our web site: TruthInHeart.com

Alethea In Heart

8071 Main St.

Fenwick, MI 48834

(989) 637-4179

FOREWORD BY THE EDITOR.

This new edition of *Mental Philosophy* was transcribed from the original 1882 Chicago edition published by S. C. Griggs and Co. All the punctuation and spelling have been retained. No changes have been made to the text. This is the second Alethea In Heart publication of this title; and is number II of the twenty volume series titled, *The Life and Works of Asa Mahan*. When completed, each volume will be available in both hard and soft covers. A similar series, called *The Life and Works of Charles G. Finney*, is also being produced by Alethea In Heart[1]. These two series compliment each other. Other series and individual works by contemporaries of Mahan, such as the sixteen volume bible commentaries by fellow Oberlin professor Henry Cowles, are also being reproduced.[2] All these reproductions are part of a massive historical project that will help scholars and people know the religious, philosophical, social, and political influences on nineteenth century English and American people.

As the relevant question is frequently asked, In which *order* should Mahan's and Finney's books be read? a recommendation will be given. When the editor first began to study Finney, it was not long before he started studying his 1851 edition of *Systematic Theology*.[3] He was not far into that volume before he read the following statements:[4]

"Let no one despair in commencing the book, nor stumble at the definitions, thinking that he can never understand so abstruse a subject. Remember that what follows is an expansion and an explanation by way of application, *of what you find so condensed in the first pages of the book.*[5] My brother, sister, friend—read, study,

---

[1] See the last page of this volume for details.

[2] Other series being worked on of contemporary authors include the works of John Fletcher, A. M. Hills, James B. Walker, and Henry Clay Trumbull.

[3] *Lectures on Systematic Theology, etc.,* London ed., 1851, published in two volumes by Alethea In Heart in 2001, 2003, and in the new 2005 series, *Life and Works of Charles G. Finney,* Vol. VI and VII.

[4] In the Preface and chapter I.

[5] This is chapter I and deals with psychology: *Various classes of truths, and how*

think, and read again. You were made to think. It will do you good to think; to develope your powers by study. God designed that religion should require thought, intense thought, and should thoroughly develope our powers of thought. The Bible itself is written in a style so condensed as to require much intense study. Many know nothing of the Bible or of religion, because they will not think and study. I do not pretend to so explain theology as to dispense with the labour of thinking. I have no ability and no wish to do so. . .

"*Theology is so related to psychology, that the successful study of the former without a knowledge of the latter, is impossible.* Every theological system, and every theological opinion, assumes something as true in psychology. Theology is, to a great extent, the science of mind in its relations to moral law. God is a mind or spirit: all moral agents are in his image. Theology is the doctrine of God, comprehending his existence, attributes, relations, character, works, word, government providential and moral, and, of course, it must embrace the facts of human nature, and the science of moral agency. *All theologians do and must assume the truth of some system of psychology and mental philosophy, and those who exclaim most loudly against metaphysics, no less than others.* . . .

"I must assume that you possess some knowledge of psychology, and of mental philosophy, and leave to your convenience a more thorough and extended examination of the subject but hinted at in this lecture."

The editor was not familiar with psychology and did find the volume difficult to grasp. This difficulty, along with the above quoted words, lead the editor to seek out such works on psychology. This lead to learning about the curriculum of the early Oberlin institution where Finney taught theology for 40 years, and to Asa Mahan (1799-1889), the first president and teacher of mental philosophy at Oberlin. Mahan wrote eight volumes, and many more papers, on psychology and related subjects—as well as many others on different subjects.[6] From around 1835 to 1850 many of Finney's theology students were also under Mahan's instruction in mental philosophy. Both men admittedly shared nearly identical views in theology and philosophy. It is fair to say that one who is familiar with even a few of those books would understand every

---

the mind attains to a knowledge of them. Emphasis added.
[6] All his books are listed at the beginning of this book.

word and concept mentioned in the opening chapter of Finney's *Systematic Theology*. And as Finney claims, once that is understood, the rest follows relatively easy.

Mahan's *Mental Philosophy* is similar to Finney's *Lecture Notes on Theology*.[7] The latter deals much more with theology and the preparation for studying theology than the former. But a comparison of the two will reveal an identical mental philosophy.

Mental Philosophy was written twenty-eight years after Mahan wrote his second edition of *Intellectual Philosophy*.[8] Both volumes cover the same intellectual material, but the latter, being almost twice the size, gives more detail. The former also covers the Sensibilities and the Will,[9] while the later covers the idea of God, immortality, and a short analysis of modern philosophical systems.[10] The former can be understood by high school students, but the later is a little more advanced. The difficulty in understanding either volume may stem from a lack of familiarity with the words, and a lack of exercise of the mind in reflection. All the books in this series require the reader to think long and deep. For a thorough study of Mahan's system of philosophy it is suggested that these two books be studied alongside of Finney's *Lecture Notes on Theology*. These will help people not familiar with philosophy to understand the more advanced books like *Logic*,[11] *A Critical History of Philosophy*, and *Natural Theology*.[12]

The former books are not only foundational for understanding the more advanced Mahan and Finney works, but also for understanding their actions as Revivalists and Reformers. Their actions were consistent with the philosophy of *Realism* as revealed in such

---

[7] *Lecture Notes on Theology; Or Introductory Lectures for the Study of Theology*. By Charles G. Finney, Fenwick, MI., Alethea In Heart, 2005.

[8] *A System of Intellectual Philosophy*, 1854 ed., Vol. III of the new series, *The Life and Works of Asa Mahan*, Alethea In Heart, 2005.

[9] Mahan's second book, *Doctrine of the Will*, 1847 ed., Vol. I, Alethea In Heart, 2005, enlarges upon what is only outlined in *Mental Philosophy*.

[10] Which became the entire subject-matter of the later volume, *A Critical History of Philosophy in two Volumes*, 1883 ed., Vol. VI and VII in the new 2005 series.

[11] *The Science of Logic; Or, An Analysis of the Laws of Thought*, 1857 ed., Vol. IV in the new 2005 series.

[12] *The Science of Natural Theology*, 1867 ed., Vol. VIII, in the new series.

books. They studied and taught philosophy, science, theology, and the Bible with a *commonsense* approach. They expected people to assume nothing as real that was not, and to also not ignore anything that was. For example, they *examined* the plain promises in the Bible about full salvation from sin through the work of Christ, and they *believed* the credible testimony of God. They also did not assume that the then present state of morals in society was beyond change or improvement, so they set out to influence and reform it by means of education, preaching, and their example.

To understand and appreciate Finney's and Mahan's theology, methods, and success as evangelists, philosophers, and reformers, the editor recommends the following order of books in the two new Alethea In Heart series: *Lectures on Revivals of Religion,*[13] and *Narrative of Revivals,*[14] by Finney, together with *Autobiography,*[15] and *Out of Darkness Into Light,*[16] and *Doctrine of the Will,* by Mahan; followed by *Lecture Notes on Theology,* by Finney, together with *Mental Philosophy* and *Intellectual Philosophy,* by Mahan; followed by *The Science of Logic,* by Mahan, with *Skeletons of a Course of Theological Lectures,*[17] by Finney; followed by Finney's *Systematic Theology,* with Mahan's *Moral Philosophy;*[18] Finally, *A Critical History of Philosophy,* and *Natural Theology,* by Mahan. The many volumes of sermons and holiness topics could be read along side all of the above mentioned works.

Richard M. Friedrich, *January* 2005.

[13] *Lectures on Revivals of Religion,* 1868 ed., Vol. I, 2005.
[14] *Narrative of Revivals, or The Revival Memoirs of Charles G. Finney,* 1869, Vol. II, 2005.
[15] *Autobiography: Intellectual, Moral, and Spiritual.* 1882 ed., Vol. IX, 2005.
[16] *Out of Darkness Into Light; Or, The Hidden Life made manifest through Facts of Observation and Experience: Facts Elucidated by the Word of God.* 1877 ed., Vol. XII, 2005.
[17] *Skeletons of a Course of Theological Lectures,* 1840 ed., Vol. III, 2005.
[18] *Science of Moral Philosophy.* 1848 ed., Vol. V, 2004.

PREFACE.

THE object of the following treatise is to furnish, not only for College classes, but especially for our Academies and High Schools a *complete* system of Mental Science. Two facts render the treatises in common use unadapted, particularly to the two purposes last named. Such treatises, in the first place, are too large for common use. Then, with hardly any exceptions, they treat of but one department of the mind, the Intellect. The object of the following treatise is to remedy both these defects—to furnish a work sufficiently ample for a clear elucidation of the whole subject, and, at the same time, so concise as not to over burden the mind of the pupil, on the one hand, and, on the other, to furnish a *full* knowledge of the *entire* system of Mental Science, the Philosophy, not of the Intellect merely, but also of the Sensibility and Will. It is fully believed by the Author, and he states this as the result of some thirty years' experience in teaching the science, that every pupil, not only in our College classes, but every advanced student in our Academies and High Schools, is capable of fully mastering this treatise, and that when he has done so, he will have attained not only to a distinct understanding of the different faculties of the mind, but also of the varied functions of each of those faculties.

An important suggestion, to teachers of this work, might not be out of place. The success of the pupil in mastering the science, will depend mainly upon the attainment of a clear understanding of the *preliminary* definitions and elucidations. Short lessons, and careful explanations, should be given here. When the pupil has fully comprehended the work, as far as to the close of the discussions of the Primary Intellectual faculties, he will pass through the remaining portions with increasing interest and delight. With these suggestions, the work is commended to the candid judgment of all who are qualified to understand and appreciate the subject.

THE AUTHOR.

9

ANALYSIS.

GENERAL INTRODUCTION.

CHAPTER I.
PRINCIPLES OF INDUCTION AND CLASSIFICATION.

CHAPTER II.
CLASSIFICATION OF MENTAL PHENOMENA AND FACULTIES.

PART I.
THE INTELLECT.

CHAPTER I.
INTELLECTUAL PHENOMENA.

11

CHAPTER II.
PRIMARY FACULTIES.

CHAPTER III.
CONSCIOUSNESS.

CHAPTER IV.
SENSE.

CHAPTER V.
REASON.

CHAPTER VIII.
ASSOCIATION.

CHAPTER XI.
REASON RESUMED.

CHAPTER XII.
LAWS OF INVESTIGATION.

PART III.
THE WILL.

A

SYSTEM OF MENTAL PHILOSOPHY.

GENERAL INTRODUCTION.

CHAPTER I.

PRINCIPLES OF INDUCTION AND CLASSIFICATION IN RESPECT TO FACTS OF MIND.

The principles of induction and classification to which the strictest adherence will be maintained, in all our inquiries, are the following: 1. No facts of mind, facts given in Consciousness, as real, will be omitted, or disregarded; and none will be supposed, or adduced as the basis of deductions, not thus given as real. 2. Phenomena, or facts, in their essential characteristics unlike, will be separated, or ranged together in distinct and opposite classes; while all facts, in their essential characteristics alike, will be ranked together in the same class. These are the principles which do, in fact, universally obtain in all other sciences, and must obtain in developing the science of mind, as the immutable condition, of reaching any valid deductions.

PRINCIPLES BY WHICH THE NATURE, CHARACTER AND NUMBER, OF THE FACULTIES AND SUSCEPTIBILITIES OF THE MIND ARE TO BE OBTAINED.

The general principle by which the nature, character, and number of the faculties, and susceptibilities of the mind are to be determined, is this: as are the diverse facts of mind, such are its diverse Faculties, and Susceptibilities. As are the essential characteristics of any particular class of facts, such is the nature of the particular faculty or susceptibility to which said facts are referred. From this general principle so obviously valid that none will question it, three general principles arise, to wit: 1. All facts whose essential characteristics are the same, are to be referred to one and the same, faculty, or susceptibility. 2. Facts fundamentally dissimilar in their nature, are to be referred to distinct and separate faculties, or susceptibilities. 3. The number of these distinct and separate Faculties and Susceptibilities is as the number of the distinct and separate classes of mental phenomena given in consciousness.

PRINCIPLES BY WHICH WE ARE TO DETERMINE THE LAWS OF MIND, THEIR
NUMBER AND CHARACTER.

The *laws of mind* are those principles in conformity to which its diverse faculties act, or are controlled. By these laws, we explain the phenomena of mind, and the action of its diverse faculties and susceptibilities. Any hypothesis, to lay claim to the high prerogative of a Law of Mind, must possess the following characteristics: 1. It must *consist,* or be consistent with, *all* the facts referred to it. Any hypothesis, undeniably contradicted by any one fundamental fact of consciousness, can have no claim to be regarded as a law of mind. 2. Said hypothesis must not only be consistent with all these facts, but must fully explain them all. A manifest failure to explain a single essential fact, annihilates utterly the claim of any hypothesis to be regarded as a law of mind. 3. These facts must be explicable upon no other actual or conceivable hypothesis. Facts equally consistent with two or more distinct and opposite hypotheses, affirm, and can affirm, neither, in distinction from the other, as a law of mind. But, when any hypothesis undeniably possesses the three characteristics above designated, it then stands demonstrably revealed, as such a law. By an undeviating adherence, in our classifications and deductions, to all the principles which we have laid down, we shall find ourselves, in all our inquiries, on the high road to certain knowledge, and shall ever enjoy, in all our leading deductions, the inward satisfaction and assurance that we can not be wrong.

CHAPTER II.

CLASSIFICATION OF MENTAL PHENOMENA AND FACULTIES.

Universal Mind has distinguished, and recognized, three classes of mental phenomena, each of which is entirely distinct from either of the others. These phenomena, which comprehend all operations of the mind, actual or conceivable, may be expressed and represented by the terms; thinking, feeling, and willing. If we attempt to form a conception of any operation of the mind whatever, we must conceive of it, as a thought, or a feeling, or an act of willing or mental determination. This, then, is a full and distinct classification of the operations of the mind, operations to be taken into account in developing the Science of Mental Philosophy, a classification which will be fully verified by the following considerations:

CLASSIFICATION VERIFIED.

1. These classes of phenomena differ from one another, not in *degree,* but in *kind.* Thought, in all degrees, whether clear or obscure, remains totally, and equally, distinct from feeling in all its forms, such as sensations, emotions, and desires, on the one hand, and all acts of willing of every kind and degree, such as choice, purpose, volition or intention, on the other. So of feeling, in respect to thought, and acts of willing of every actual or conceivable kind and degree. Nor is willing in one degree, a thought; in another, a sensation, emotion, or desire; and in another still, a choice, purpose, volition, or intention. In all degrees and modifications, these three classes of mental operations, or phenomena, remain equally distinct, in their nature and fundamental characteristics.

2. This classification is, also, verified by the testimony of universal Consciousness. When, for example, one speaks of *thinking* of any particular object, then of *desiring* it, and lastly of having *determined* to secure the object, all mankind in common, at once,

apprehend his meaning in each of these statements, and understand him as referring to three entirely distinct classes of mental operations. No one, when spoken to of thought, feeling, or willing, in any of their forms, ever confounds any one of these states with either of the others.

3. In all languages, there are distinct *terms* appropriated to express and represent each of these three classes of mental phenomena, terms, each of which is exclusively appropriated to one class, and never applied to either of the others. No one, for example, ever employs the term *thought* to represent feeling, that is sensation, emotion, or desire, or any act of willing. The same holds equally true of the terms feeling and willing. Each, by universal usage, represents one class of phenomena, and is never employed to represent either of the others.

4. Qualifying terms are also in common use, terms which are exclusively applied to each of these classes of phenomena, and never to either of the others. Thus, for example, we are accustomed to speak of *clear thoughts,* but never of clear feelings, or determinations. We speak of *inflexible purposes,* but never of inflexible feelings or thoughts. We also speak of *irrepressible emotions* and desires, but never of irrepressible thoughts or determinations

5. The threefold distinction and classification of mental phenomena now under consideration, is clearly marked by universal mind, and is now so generally recognized in treatises on mental science, that nothing further upon the subject is demanded in this connection. Without the presentation of any additional considerations, therefore, we will now proceed to an enumeration of the mental faculties implied by this classification of mental phenomena.

MENTAL FACULTIES IMPLIED BY THIS CLASSIFICATION.

The threefold division and classification of mental phenomena above presented, most clearly and undeniably imply a corresponding division and classification of the Mental Faculties, Functions, or Powers, a division and classification which, in accordance with general usage, we shall represent by the terms; Intellect or

Intelligence, Sensibility or Sensitivity, and Will. To the first faculty, we refer all the phenomena of thought, in all its forms. To the second we refer all feelings, such as sensations, emotions, and desires; and to the last, all acts of willing, or mental determinations. The science of mind, consequently, divides itself into three parts, a development of the phenomena and laws of the Intellect,—of the Sensibility—and of Will.

MEANING OF THE WORDS, MENTAL FACULTIES.

When we speak of a diversity of mental faculties, we would by no means, be understood, as holding, or as teaching, the wild dogma, that mind, like the body, is made up of parts which may be separated from one another. Mind is not constituted of a diversity of blended substances. It is one substance not susceptible of division. Yet this one substance is capable of a diversity of functions, or operations, which are entirely distinct from one another. This diversity of capabilities, all of which pertain to this one substance, we designate by the words, Mental Faculties, and hence, the phenomena being distinct and separate from one another, we speak of the powers and susceptibilities of thought, feeling, and willing, as distinct and separate faculties of the mind, faculties which we designate, as stated, by the terms; Intellect, Sensibility, and Will. The observations made above in respect to the mind itself, will, at once, appear equally applicable to each, of the mental faculties above enumerated. As we speak of the Intelligence, for example, as a faculty of the mind entirely distinct from the Sensibility and Will, without implying that the mind is not one substance, so we may speak of the diverse Faculties of the Intellect without implying that that faculty is a compound of a diversity of parts. The term Faculty, whether applied to the whole mind, or to any department of the same, implies a diversity of functions of this one identical substance, not a diversity of substances, or parts.

PART I.

THE INTELLECT.

CHAPTER I.

INTELLECTUAL PHENOMENA.

The sphere of Mental Science, as indicated in the preceding chapter, includes in itself three fundamental departments of inquiry —the Science of the Intellect—the Doctrine of the Will—and an analysis of the Sensibilities of the Mind. Part I. of the present treatise will be occupied with the Science of the Intellect, or with a development of the *Phenomena, Faculties, and Laws of the Human Intelligence.* The present chapter will be occupied, in accordance with the principles of true science, with a classification of THE PHENOMENA OF THE INTELLIGENCE. As all that we know, or can know, of this, as well as of every other department of the mind, is revealed to us through the phenomena which lie under the eye of Consciousness, the first inquiries which now present themselves are: What are the phenomena of thought thus revealed? What are their fundamental characteristics? In conformity to what principles shall they be classified and arranged?

PRINCIPLE OF CLASSIFICATION.

There is one principle, in conformity to which all intellectual phenomena may be properly classified, and in the light of which, the fundamental characteristics of such phenomena may be very distinctly presented. We refer to the *modes* in which all objects of thought are conceived of by the intelligence. Of these modes, there are two entirely distinct and separate, the one from the other. Every

29

object of thought is conceived of as existing either contingently or of necessity: that is, that object is conceived of as existing, with the possibility of *conceiving* of its nonexistence, or it is conceived of as existing with the impossibility of conceiving of its non-existence. If we have any conceptions of an object at all we must conceive of it as falling under one or the other of these relations. The principle of classification, therefore, is fundamental, and of universal application.

CONTINGENT AND NECESSARY PHENOMENA OF THOUGHT DEFINED.

Every thought, conception, cognition, or idea, then, by whatever term we may choose to designate it, all the phenomena of the Intelligence, may be classed as contingent or necessary. A conception is *contingent,* when its OBJECT may be conceived of as existing with the possibility of conceiving of its non-existence.

An idea is *necessary* when its OBJECT is conceived of as existing with the impossibility of conceiving of its nonexistence. All the phenomena of the intelligence must, as shown above, fall under one or the other of these relations. It remains now, to illustrate the principle of classification here adopted, by a reference to an adequate number of particular phenomena, as the basis of important distinctions pertaining to the different functions or powers of the intelligence. In the notice which we shall take of particular phenomena, other important characteristics, aside from those under consideration, will be developed, while these will be kept prominently in mind as the grounds of classification.

IDEA OF BODY CONTINGENT.

We will begin with the idea of body. Take any one body we please, the book, for an example, which lies before us. While we conceive of this body, as existing, we can also, with perfect readiness, conceive its non-existence. We believe that the time was, when it had no existence, and that the time may come, when it will cease to exist. The power which brought it into being, may also annihilate it. The same holds true of all bodies, of every kind. All objects around us, the world itself, and the entire universe, we contemplate as existing with the possibility of, at the same time, conceiving of their non-existence. They do exist. They may be conceived of as not existing. There is no difficulty of conceiving of these propositions as true. Nor is there any perceived contradiction between them. The idea of body then is contingent. We always conceive of the object of that idea as existing, with the possibility of, at the same time, conceiving of its non-existence.

IDEA OF SPACE NECESSARY.

We now turn to a consideration of the idea of space. We can, as shown above, readily conceive of the annihilation of all bodies, of the universe itself. But when we have conceived of this, can we conceive that space, in which the universe exists, may be annihilated? We cannot. We conceive of space as a reality, as really existing. Can we conceive of it as not being? We cannot. No intelligent being can form such a conception. Of this everyone is perfectly conscious. When we have conceived of the nonexistence of this world, and of all other bodies, of the entire universe itself, let any one attempt to conceive of the annihilation of space, in which we necessarily conceive of all these objects as existing, and he will find the formation of such a conception, an absolute impossibility. The idea of space then is necessary. We conceive of the object of that idea as existing, with the impossibility of conceiving of its non-existence.

IDEAS OF SUCCESSION, AND TIME, OR DURATION.

These ideas are in all intelligent minds. No individual, whose intelligence has been developed at all, will fail to understand you, when you speak of one event, as having happened; of another, as having succeeded it; and of the fact that that succession took place in some definite period of time. We will now mark the characteristic of these ideas.

IDEA OF SUCCESSION CONTINGENT.

You can conceive of some one event as having happened, and of another as having succeeded it. In other words, you have the

31

idea of succession. Can you not *conceive,* that neither of these events occurred? Every individual can readily form such a conception. The same holds true of all events, of all succession of every kind, and in all time. The idea of succession, like that of body, is therefore contingent.

THE IDEA OF THE NECESSARY.

But when we have conceived of the total cessation of succession, we find it absolutely impossible to conceive that there is no time, or duration, in which succession may take place. We can no more conceive of the annihilation of time, than we can of that of space. The idea of time, then, like that of space, is necessary.

IDEAS OF THE FINITE AND OF THE INFINITE.

The ideas of Space and Duration, as they exist in all minds, not only bear the characteristics of necessity, but each, in common, pertains to its object as absolutely *infinite.* This is undeniable. The ideas of body and succession, each pertains to its object, as limitable or finite. Those of space and duration pertain to their objects, as being without limits, or as infinite. Each of these ideas, that of the finite on the one hand, and of the infinite on the other, may be detached from the objects to which they pertain, and be considered by itself. These ideas then whatever philosophers of certain schools, may say to the contrary, are, undeniably, in the mind. They are also distinct, the one from the other. Consequently the one cannot be derived from the other. The multiplication of the finite cannot give the infinite. Nor by dividing the infinite do we find the finite. Being correlative ideas, the one necessarily supposes and suggests the other. The one cannot possibly exist in the mind without the other. Yet, as above remarked, the one is perfectly distinct from the other.

Nor is one of these ideas less *distinct* than the other. When I speak of the infinite, every one as readily and distinctly apprehends my meaning, as when I speak of the finite. The following propositions, for example—body is limitable; space is illimitable—are equally intelligible to all minds.

There are other forms in which these ideas appear in the mind, in all of which they sustain, to each other, the same relations, and possess the same characteristics. When the mind conceives of power, wisdom or goodness, as imperfect or limited, or finite, it necessarily conceives of attributes of the same class as perfect, unlimited, or infinite: just as when it conceives of a reality which is and began to be, it necessarily conceives of a reality which, not only is, but always was.

If an individual still affirms that he has no idea of the infinite, we have only to ask him whether he understands the import of the words he employs, when he makes such an affirmation: whether he is not conscious of speaking of something, which, in thought, he himself clearly distinguishes from all that is limitable, or limited. These questions, he will readily answer in the affirmative. In this answer he clearly contradicts the affirmation under consideration. For, if he really, as he affirms, has no idea of the infinite, he would not know the meaning of the terms he uses, nor could he, in thought, clearly distinguish the infinite, from all that is limitable, or finite.

If also we have no real or positive idea of the infinite, we can have none of time and space, for they are positive ideas, and their objects are given in the intelligence, as positively, or absolutely, infinite.

IDEAS OF MENTAL PHENOMENA AND PERSONAL IDENTITY.

Every individual believes, and must believe, that he is now the same being that he was yesterday, and will be tomorrow. Numberless, and ever varying phenomena are constantly passing under the eye of consciousness. Many are recalled of which we were formerly conscious. Yet they are all referred to the same individual subject. All phenomena, of thought, feeling, and willing, of which we are now conscious, which we recall, as having in some former period, been conscious of, or which we expect to put forth in some future time, are given in the intelligence in this exclusive form—I think, I feel, I will; I did think, I did feel, I did

33

will so and so. The same holds equally true of all similar phenomena which we contemplate, as about to occur in future time. Whatever the phenomena may be, the same identical I is given as its subject. This is what is meant by personal identity. It is the *unity of our being,* of the *I or self,* as opposed to the plurality and ever changing phenomena of consciousness. Having shown that the idea of mental phenomena and of personal identity are in the mind, we will consider their characteristics.

IDEA OF MENTAL PHENOMENA CONTINGENT AND RELATIVE.

An idea is said to be relative, when its object can be conceived as existing, but upon the condition, that some other object is conceived of as, also, existing. Thus, for example, we cannot conceive body to exist, without conceiving of space as existing. The reality of succession, also, implies that of time. The ideas of body and succession, therefore, are not only contingent, but also relative ideas. The same, as we shall perceive hereafter, holds true of the ideas of phenomena and events, and we might add of all other contingent ideas.

You have a consciousness of some thought, feeling, or act of will. You remember similar phenomena of which you were formerly conscious. You conceive of them as now being, or as having been, actual realities. Can you not conceive of them as not being or as never having taken place? You can. Can you conceive of such phenomena as existing or having existed, without referring them to some subject? In other words, can you conceive of some thought, feeling, or volition as now existing, or as having existed in former times, without referring it to some subject, some being which thinks, feels, or wills? You cannot. All the phenomena of consciousness are, contingent and relative.

IDEA OF PERSONAL IDENTITY NECESSARY.

How is it with the idea of personal identity? You are now conscious of some thought or feeling, or act of will. You recall others, of a similar nature, of which you have been formerly conscious. This you refer to one and the same subject, the I of

34

consciousness, as it is sometimes called. This reference you and all mankind alike must make. This reference mankind universally make in all the transactions of life. Under its influence we hold ourselves and others bound to fulfill contracts made years ago. Under its influence, the virtuous are commended and rewarded, and the vicious are blamed and punished for actions long since performed. Under its influence we anticipate the retributions of eternal justice in a future state for the deeds done in the body. Is it possible to avoid making this reference? It is not. You cannot possibly conceive of a thought, for example, without referring it to some subject which thinks. You cannot be conscious of any mental phenomenon, or recall any others of which you were formerly conscious, without referring them to one and the same subject, yourself. The idea of personal identity, then, is necessary.

NECESSARY IDEAS DISTINGUISHED AS CONDITIONAL AND UNCONDITIONAL.

Here an important distinction between necessary ideas demands special attention. When we contemplate the ideas of space and duration, for example, we find that the objects of these ideas must exist, whether anything else exists or not. Those ideas, therefore, are not only necessary, but unconditioned and absolute. On the other hand, the ideas of personal identity, and of substance and cause which we shall hereafter consider, are not, in this sense, necessary. They are only conditionally necessary. Phenomena being given, substance must be. An event being given, the supposition of a cause is necessary. Phenomena and events not being given, we do not affirm the existence of substances or causes. The phenomena of consciousness not being given, we do not affirm the reality or identity of the self, the subject of these phenomena. Such ideas are conditionally necessary, and not like those of space and time, not only necessary, but unconditioned and absolute.

IDEAS OF PHENOMENA AND SUBSTANCE.—IDEA OF SUBSTANCE EXPLAINED.

If the observations which have been made upon the idea of personal identity, have been distinctly understood, the characteristics of the idea of substance will be readily apprehended. All the phenomena of consciousness and memory are, as we have seen, by a necessary law of our being, referred to one and the same subject. The phenomena are accidents, perpetually changing. The subject, however, remains the same. Now, in the language of Cousin, "Being, one and identical, opposed to variable accidents, to transitory phenomena, is Substance." But thus far we have only personal substance. The same principle however, applies equally to all external substances. Through the medium of our senses, such objects are given to us as being possessed of a great variety of qualities, and as existing in a great variety of states. The qualities and states, which are perpetually varying, we necessarily refer to one and the same subject; a subject which remains one and identical, and the endlessly diversified phenomena which it exhibits. This is substance.

IDEA OF PHENOMENA CONTINGENT AND RELATIVE.—THAT OF SUBSTANCE NECESSARY.

Now as it is with our ideas of the phenomena of consciousness and personal identity, so it is with our ideas of external phenomena and external substance. The former is contingent and relative; the latter is necessary. When any phenomenon appears, we can readily conceive that it had not appeared. Its appearance also we can admit, only on the supposition of something else, to wit, substance, to which this appearance is necessarily referred. Our ideas of phenomena, therefore, are contingent and relative.

On the other hand, the idea of substance, relatively to phenomena, is necessary. Phenomena being given, substance *must* be. It is impossible for us to conceive of the former without the latter.

IDEAS OF SUBSTANCE NOT OBSCURE, BUT CLEAR AND DISTINCT.

According to Locke, "We have no clear idea of substance in general." This idea, also, he represents, as "of little use in philosophy." In reply, it may be said, that our idea of substance is just as clear and important, as those of time, space, and personal identity. Of this every one is conscious. The same function of the intelligence which apprehends one of these ideas, apprehends them all. Take away the power to apprehend one, and the power to apprehend every other of these ideas is annihilated. Philosophy itself also becomes an impossibility. How could we reason philosophically about ourselves, in the absence of the idea of personal identity? Equally impossible would it be, to reason about objects external to us, in the absence of the idea of substance. This and kindred ideas, instead of being "of little use in philosophy," are, in reality, the foundation of all our explanations of phenomena, external and internal.

We often hear individuals, in expatiating upon the great ignorance of man, affirming, that all we "know of realities in and around us, is their phenomena. Of the substances themselves, we know nothing." In reply to such rhapsodies, it may be said, that our knowledge of every substance of every kind, is just as clear, distinct, and extensive, as our knowledge of its phenomena. In phenomena, substances stand revealed, the substance being as its phenomena. In the phenomena of thought, for example, we know ourselves, as thinking beings, or substances, our powers being as the thoughts which they generate. Our knowledge of the powers of thought, is just as distinct as that of thought itself. The same holds true in respect to all substances, material and mental.

IDEAS OF EVENTS AND CAUSE.

The universe within and around us, presents the constant spectacle of endlessly diversified and ever changing phenomena. Some of these are constantly conjoined, in the relation of "immediate and invariable antecedence and consequence." The connection between others is only occasional. In reference to events of the former class, the mind judges, that the relation between them is, not only that of antecedent and consequence, but of cause and effect. In reference to every event, however, whether its antecedent is perceived or not, we judge that it had a cause. This judgment is universal, extending to all events, actual and conceivable. It is absolutely impossible for us to conceive of an event without a cause. Let any one make the effort to form such a conception, and he will find that he has attempted an impossibility. Here it should be noticed, that we do not affirm that every *effect* has a cause. That would be mere tautology. It would be equivalent to the affirmation, that whatever is produced by a cause, is produced by a cause. All this might be true, and the proposition, every event has a cause, be false, notwithstanding.

THE IDEA OF EVENTS CONTINGENT AND RELATIVE.—THAT OF CAUSE NECESSARY.

The relation between the idea of an event, and that of a cause, may be readily pointed out. Whenever the mind witnesses, or is conscious of, the occurrence of an event, it apprehends that event as contingent and relative. It might or might not have happened. There is no impossibility in making these different suppositions. The occurrence of an event also necessarily supposes something else, to wit, a cause. On the other hand, no event uncaused can possibly be conceived to have taken place. The idea of an event, then, is contingent and relative. The idea of cause is necessary, conditionally so, as shown above.

IDEA OF POWER.

The idea of Power, is that of causation in its quiescent state, or as the permanent attribute of a subject irrespective of its action, at any particular moment. When particular effects are attributed to particular causes, while the nature of the substances containing such causes remains unchanged, the mind considers the power to repeat such effects under the same circumstances, as the *permanent* attribute of those substances. This is the idea of power, as it exists in all minds. All substances, in their active state, are Causes—in their quiescent state, are Powers. Powers are of two kinds, active and passive. The latter are commonly called susceptibilities. As the existence of powers and causes is indicated by their respective phenomena, so the nature of such powers and causes is indicated by the characteristics of their respective phenomena.

The idea of power, sustaining as it does, the same relation to phenomena, that that of cause and substance do, is, of course, like those ideas, universal and necessary.

CONCLUSION OF THE PRESENT ANALYSIS.

Here our analysis of intellectual phenomena will close, for the present. It might have been extended to almost any length. Enough has been said, however, to indicate the principle of classification adopted, and to show its universal applicability, as well as to lay the foundation for the important distinctions, etc., in respect to the intellectual powers, an elucidation of which will be begun in the next chapter.

CHAPTER II.

APPLICATION OF THE PRECEDING ANALYSIS.— PRIMARY INTELLECTUAL FACULTIES. — PERCEIVED AND IMPLIED ELEMENTS OF THOUGHT.

All the elements of thought, all ideas and conceptions, existing in the mind, may, as we have seen, be classed, as contingent, or necessary. In other words, all objects of thought are, or may be, in fact, conceived of as existing, with the possibility of conceiving of them as not existing, or with the *impossibility* of conceiving of their non-existence, that is, as being unconditionally, or conditionally necessary.

On careful reflection, it will be perceived, that all contingent elements of thought are given exclusively by *perception,* external or internal, their objects being recognized by the universal intelligence, as objects of perception. The necessary elements, on the other hand, are not recognized by the intelligence as given by perception, but as distinctly and immediately *implied* by what we perceive. Thus, for example, body, succession, phenomena external and internal, and events, are objects of perception, and are so recognized by the universal intelligence. The ideas of space, time, substance, and cause, on the other hand, are not recognized by the consciousness, as given by perception, but as *implied* by the ideas of body, succession, phenomena, and events, which are given, as objects of perception. Body, succession, phenomena, and events, we *perceive.* Space, duration, substance, and causes, we do not perceive, but *apprehend* as implied by the realities which we do perceive. No one will question the correctness of these statements.

THE ELEMENTS OF ALL FORMS OF REAL KNOWLEDGE DERIVED FROM THESE TWO SOURCES.

All forms of knowledge, all ideas, and conceptions, existing in the mind, are constituted of elements derived originally from these two sources exclusively, to wit, what we perceive, and what is

40

necessarily and immediately implied by what we perceive. Knowledge, in any other form, or from any other source, is inconceivable, and naturally impossible.

LOGICAL AND CHRONOLOGICAL ORDER OF THESE FORMS OF KNOWLEDGE.

There are two fundamental relations which all forms of perceived and implied knowledge, that is, contingent and necessary ideas, sustain to each other, relations which it is very important, that the learner should fully comprehend. We refer to what is denominated the *logical* and *chronological* order of such ideas.

THE LOGICAL ORDER.

One idea is the logical antecedent of another, when the former is implied by the latter, that is, when the reality of the *object* of the latter can be admitted, but on the supposition of the reality of the *object* of the former. Body, for example, cannot exist unless space does exist. Succession is possible but on the condition of the reality of duration in which the former does and must occur, if it occur at all. Unless real substances and causes do exist, there can, by no possibility, be any such thing, as phenomena, or events. The ideas of space, duration, substance, and cause, consequently are the logical antecedents of the ideas of body, succession, phenomena, and events. In other words, implied forms of knowledge, or necessary ideas, are the logical antecedents of forms of perceived knowledge, or of contingent ideas. This principle universally obtains.

THE CHRONOLOGICAL ORDER.

One idea is the chronological antecedent of another, when, in the order of actual *origination* in the mind, the former precedes the latter. In this order, the perceived universally precedes the implied. In other words, contingent ideas, are universally, the chronological antecedents of the necessary. We perceive body, before we apprehend space in which the former does and must exist. We perceive succession, before we apprehend duration in which, the former occurs. We perceive phenomena and events, before we do, or can, apprehend substance and cause to which the former are

41

referred. The truth of these statements is demonstrably evident. Space is apprehended and can be conceived of, or defined, but as that in which body, and substances, do and must exist, and as implied by the same. Duration, or time, is apprehended, and can be conceived of, or defined, but as the place of succession, and as implied by it. Substance, or cause, is apprehended but as that to which phenomena, or events, are referred, and as implied by the same. Now that which is, and can be, apprehended but as related to, and implied by, some other object, cannot, by any possibility, be to the mind, an object of knowledge, prior to that by which it is implied, and known only as implied. Knowledge by perception, therefore is, and must be, in the order of origination in the mind, prior to implied knowledge. In other words, contingent ideas are, universally, the chronological antecedents of necessary ideas. This principle, as we shall see, hereafter, is of fundamental importance in the science of mind.

PRIMARY INTELLECTUAL FACULTIES.

All knowledge begins, and undeniably so, with perception, and is instantly followed by, and blended with, those forms, and elements, of knowledge directly and immediately implied by what is obtained by perception, and from these two sources, we repeat, the constituent elements of all human knowledge, of all ideas and conceptions, in the mind, are originally derived. The organs of perceived and implied knowledge, therefore, are the *Primary Faculties* of the Intelligence. This is undeniable.

KNOWLEDGE BY PERCEPTION CLASSIFIED.

Knowledge by perception, however, is of two distinct and separate kinds, and is derived from two distinct, and separate sources, *external* and *internal,* objective and subjective. Knowledge by perception pertains, in part, to external, material, substances, and, in part, to internal phenomena, the operations of the mind itself. We have, then, two distinct and separate faculties of perception, the external and the internal, that which perceives external, material, substances, and that which perceives internal phenomena, or the operations of the mind itself. The former, we denominate Sense, or the Faculty of External Perception. The latter we denominate Consciousness, or the Faculty Of Internal Perception. That faculty by which we apprehend implied knowledge, or the objects of necessary ideas, we denominate Reason. The following, therefore, are the primary faculties of the intelligence, namely:

PRIMARY INTELLECTUAL FACULTIES.

1. The Faculty of *internal* perception, the function of the intelligence by which we perceive and apprehend the phenomena of the mind itself. This faculty we denominate Consciousness.

2. The Faculty of *external* perception, the intellectual function by which we perceive and apprehend the qualities of external, material, substances. This faculty we denominate Sense.

3. The Faculty of *implied knowledge,* the function of the intelligence by which we apprehend necessary truths. This faculty we denominate Reason.

The terms, Consciousness, Sense, and Reason, throughout this treatise, will be employed in strict accordance with the definitions of the same above given. The definition given to the term consciousness, accords with universal usage. That given to the term sense is the first meaning assigned to it by Webster, and is the meaning generally attached to it when employed, as it is in this treatise, to designate a special faculty, or function, of the intelligence. A great diversity of meanings attach to it, when employed for other purposes. Similar, remarks apply to the term, reason. In common language, various meanings are attached to it. In scientific treatises, it is now being generally employed in strict accordance with the definition of it above given.

THESE FACULTIES—WHY CALLED PRIMARY.

Consciousness, Sense, and Reason, are called the primary faculties of the intelligence, for two considerations:

1. Because, that with them, all our knowledge commences.

2. All our complex cognitions are composed of elements given by these faculties. All the phenomena of the intelligence are either simple or complex. All simple ideas are found to be direct intuitions of one or of the other of these faculties. All complex ideas are found, on a careful analysis, to be composed of elements previously given by these faculties. The truth of this last remark will be fully confirmed in the progress of our subsequent investigations.

ALSO CALLED INTUITIVE FACULTIES.

The faculties above named are also sometimes denominated Intuitive Faculties. The reason is, that each alike pertains to its objects, by direct intuition. Consciousness, for example, by direct intuition, and not through any medium, apprehends the phenomena of the mind. The same is true of the faculty of Sense in respect to the phenomena of external material substances. The action of Reason is conditioned on the prior action of sense and consciousness. It is not through any medium, but by direct intuition, however, that reason affirms truth as universal, necessary, and absolute. Like the former, therefore, it may, with equal propriety, be denominated a faculty of intuition. These faculties, as we shall see hereafter, give us the elements of all our knowledge.

FUNDAMENTAL ERROR OF LOCKE, AND OF THE SENSUAL SCHOOL OF PHILOSOPHY.

According to Locke, and the Sensual School in philosophy, of which he was the founder, the elements of all our knowledge are derived exclusively from two sources, external, and internal, perception. "Our observation," he says, "employed either about external, sensible objects, or about the internal operations of our minds, perceived and reflected on by ourselves, is that which supplies our understanding with all the materials of thinking. These two are the fountains of knowledge from whence all the ideas we have, or can naturally have, do spring." Neither this author, nor his school in philosophy, take any account of implied knowledge, or of necessary truths, that is, knowledge by reason. They even, as seen above, deny the possibility of this form of knowledge, and take no account, whatever, of the faculty by which such knowledge is obtained. This is a fundamental error in philosophy, an error which legitimately led to the Materialism and Atheism of the latter part of the past, and early part of the present century, and which in fact lies at the foundation of much of the infidelity of the present time. Implied knowledge, or necessary ideas, is just as real, and as valid, as knowledge by perception, or as contingent ideas. When this fact is admitted, and when the validity of each of the primary faculties, as organs of real knowledge, is vindicated, there will be, in the sphere of science, no denial of the being and perfections, of a personal God, or of the truths of religion. Infidelity, in all its forms, and in all ages, has, in fact, and form, based its deductions upon a denial of the reality, or validity, of some one or other of the primary faculties above defined. In all ages and nations, and in all schools of philosophy in which the validity of knowledge through each of the primary faculties, has been admitted,—as true science immutably demands that it shall be,—the being and perfections of a personal God, and the essential truths of religion, have been universally admitted and affirmed.

FUNDAMENTAL ERROR OF THE GERMAN, OR TRANSCENDENTAL SCHOOL IN
PHILOSOPHY.

The German, or Transcendental School in Philosophy, in opposition to that of Locke, makes every thing of implied knowledge, or of necessary ideas, and takes little, or no account of knowledge by perception, external and internal, but to deny its validity. According to the fundamental principles and teachings of this, the German school, necessary ideas are originated in the mind prior to contingent ones, the former giving existence to, and determining the essential characteristics of the latter. In other words, implied knowledge exists in the mind prior to that by which the former is implied, and without the prior existence of which, the implied, can, by no possibility, as we have already seen, exist at all: one of the greatest, and most palpable, errors that ever appeared in the sphere of philosophy. Knowledge by perception, does in fact, and from the nature of the case, must, in actual experience, precede, occasion, and determine the essential characteristics of, all forms of implied knowledge. In other words, contingent elements of knowledge, instead of being preceded, occasioned, and determined in their nature and form, by the necessary elements, do, in fact, precede, occasion, and determine the fundamental characteristics of the elements of necessary ideas. It is this fundamental error of this school, which has given being and form to the Idealism, and Skepticism of the present century.

THE TRUE PHILOSOPHY.

The true philosophy, avoiding the fundamental errors of both schools,—of the Sensual, on the one hand, and of the transcendental, on the other,—and vindicating the validity of both perceived and implied knowledge in all their legitimate forms, and through each primary faculty in common, will vindicate, within the sphere of true science, the doctrine of the being and perfections of a personal God, together with the essential truths and principles of morality and religion, while it will fully meet and satisfy, all the real scientific demands of universal mind.

CHAPTER III.

CONSCIOUSNESS.

Consciousness, or the Faculty of internal Perception, has already been defined, as that faculty or function of the intelligence by which we perceive, and apprehend, the phenomena, or operations and states, of the mind itself. By consciousness we have a knowledge of all that occurs in the interior of our own minds, just as through the faculty of sense, or external perception, we know the events of the external world around us. Consciousness, as above defined, Sir William Hamilton denominates Self-Consciousness. "Internal Perception, or Self-Consciousness," he says, "is the faculty *presentative* or *intuitive* of the phenomena of the Ego or mind." It makes no difference by what name a specific faculty is called, while there is a perfect agreement in regard to its actual existence, and proper sphere and functions.

IMMEDIATE AND MEDIATE KNOWLEDGE DEFINED.

Two forms of knowledge exist in the mind, forms of knowledge which may be denominated *immediate,* and *mediate.* When we have a direct, intuitive, perception of an object, we say that we have an *immediate* knowledge of that object. When, on the other hand, we know an object, not directly and immediately, but through some other object, we then attain to a form of knowledge which is denominated *mediate knowledge.* All forms of immediate knowledge, Sir William Hamilton refers to one and the same general faculty which he denominates Consciousness, assigning to it two distinct functions, those of *external* and *internal* perception, or the faculties of Sense and Self-Consciousness. Whenever we have a direct and immediate perception of any object, we are he affirms, *conscious* of that object. If such a use of language should generally obtain, the faculty of internal perception being denominated Self-Consciousness, not a little would be gained in the sphere of distinct thought. The term *conscious* we shall employ as this

author has defined it, employing the term Consciousness according
to general usage, and as above defined.

KNOWLEDGE BY CONSCIOUSNESS DIRECT AND IMMEDIATE.

Knowledge by Consciousness is always direct and immediate.
We do not perceive, or know, our own mental states through any
medium, but are always directly and immediately conscious of the
same. This is undeniable, and is universally admitted.

KNOWLEDGE BY CONSCIOUSNESS HAS ABSOLUTE VALIDITY.

Knowledge by Consciousness, therefore, has the highest
possible validity, and within the sphere of science, must be held as
absolutely valid for the reality and character of all its respective
objects. It is "science falsely so called," that would deny, ignore, or
modify, any fact, or facts, of which we are really and truly
conscious. Facts of consciousness, and these exclusively, as the
student of mental science should keep constantly and distinctly in
mind in all his mental investigations, lie at the basis of all
legitimate deductions, throughout the entire sphere of this science.
If he would not be fundamentally misled in his inquiries, he must
immutably adhere to the principles laid down in the introduction to
this treatise, to wit, to deny, ignore, or modify, no facts actually
given in consciousness as real, to suppose or assume, as the basis
of deduction, no facts not thus given, and finally to hold, as
immutably valid, all deductions to which such real facts do
legitimately lead.

FACTS OR OBJECTS OF CONSCIOUSNESS.

In every act of consciousness, two objects are directly and
immediately cognized, or perceived and apprehended, to wit, some
particular mental state on the one hand, and the mind itself, the I,
or self, as the subject of that state, on the other; and we are just as
distinctly, and absolutely conscious of the one, as we are of the
other. Every such act, we represent in such language as the
following: I think, I feel, I will. In all such states, we are as
absolutely conscious of the I that thinks, feels, and wills, as we are

of the phenomena of thought, feeling, and willing, which we refer to the self, or the *I*. Of this, every one will be fully conscious, who will carefully reflect upon what he actually has cognizance of, in all acts of consciousness. All my mental states, I know and recognize absolutely as *my own*. How can I know them as mine unless I am conscious, and equally so, of them as mental states, and of the I, myself, as the subject of said states? "Is it not," says Mr. Mansel, "a flat contradiction to maintain that I am not immediately conscious of myself, but only of my sensations or volitions? Who then is this I that 'is conscious, and how can I be conscious of such states as MINE? In this case it would surely be far more accurate to say, not that I am conscious of my sensations, but that the sensation is conscious of itself; but thus worded, the glaring absurdity of the theory would carry with it its own refutation." Again he says: "The one *presented substance,* the source from which our data for thinking on the subject are originally drawn, is *myself.* Whatever may be the variety of the phenomena of consciousness, sensations by this or that organ, volitions, thoughts, imaginations; of all we are immediately conscious as affections of one and the same self. It is not by any afterthought of reflection that I combine together sight, thought, and volition, into a factitious unity or compounded whole; in each case I am immediately conscious of my self seeing and hearing, willing and thinking. This, self-personality, like all other simple apprehensions, is indefinable; but it is so, because it is superior to definition. It can be analyzed into no simple element, for it is itself the simplest of all; it can be made no clearer by description or comparison, for it is revealed to us in all the clearness of an original intuition, of which description and comparison can furnish only faint and partial resemblances."

THE MIND SELF-CONSCIOUS OF ITS OWN PERSONALITY.

The truth above announced is of fundamental importance in mental science, and is now being distinctly recognized as such, within the sphere of that science. We affirm ourselves to be persons, and not things, because we have a direct, immediate, and absolute consciousness of our own personality. We affirm ourselves to be persons endowed with the powers of thought, feeling, and voluntary determination, because we are absolutely conscious of ourselves, as actually exercising these diverse mental functions. We affirm our personal identity, because we are absolutely conscious of ourselves, as being the same persons to-day, that we were yesterday.

IMPORTANT ERROR IN MENTAL PHILOSOPHY.

Until quite recently, philosophers have been accustomed to distinguish between phenomena and substance in this form. They have affirmed, that the former, and not the latter, is the object of perception, external and internal.

"We are not," says Professor Stewart, "immediately conscious of its (the mind's) *existence;* but we are conscious of sensation, thought, and volition; operations which imply the existence of something which feels, thinks, and wills." Now there is no such distinction, as is here made, between phenomena and substance. Phenomena is substance itself *manifested* to the mind. The idea of appearance, where and when no substance appears, is admitted, even by Kant, to be an absolute absurdity. Appearance is nothing but substance appearing, and a sound philosophy will hold this principle, as having universal and absolute validity throughout the entire domain of science mental and physical, to wit, that *substances* IN THEIR NATURE ARE AS THEIR REAL, OR ESSENTIAL PHENOMENA. The opposite doctrine leads to the wildest conceivable absurdities, in mental science especially. Suppose, that, in accordance with the teachings of Mr. Stewart and others, thought, feeling, and volition, should appear in empty space, the subject of these phenomena not appearing in them, and consequently, manifested nowhere else, at all. How could we know who that subject is, or whether any such subject does, in fact, exist?

OBJECTION ANSWERED.

But *how,* it may be asked, can there be, at the same time, a knowledge of both the *subject,* and the *object* of knowledge? How can the mind at one and the same moment, be conscious of a given state and of itself as the subject of that state? In reply we would put to the objector two or three other questions, and when he has answered these, we will fully explain to him the *quo modo* of knowledge by Consciousness in all its forms, and through every other faculty also. *How,* we ask, in the first place, can the mind be conscious of, or know any object whatever? *How* can the mind be conscious of any mental state, and *not* be conscious of itself, as the subject of that state? In other words, how can there be phenomena, when no substance is manifested; an appearance, when no substance appears? The question to be solved by philosophy is, not *how* we know, but *what* do we know? It is not, *how* we do, or can know, but *what* we do in fact, know, by consciousness? The question, *what* do we, in fact, know by consciousness, has already been answered, to wit, our own mental states, and our own personal selves as the subject of those states. Sound philosophy will accept the answer as given, and that without any attempt to modify that answer, in fact or in form.

NATURAL OR SPONTANEOUS, AND PHILOSOPHICAL, OR REFLECTIVE CONSCIOUSNESS.

Consciousness, in its simple spontaneous form, is common to all mankind, in the natural development of their intelligence. In the language of Cousin, it is "in all men a natural process." Every individual is accustomed to use the propositions, I think, I feel, I will, etc., all persons, also, are accustomed to speak of themselves as conscious of particular states or exercises of mind. This evinces that they not only are conscious of their own mental exercises, but also are aware of the function of the intelligence exercised under such circumstances. All men, also, in the spontaneous develop- ments of consciousness, clearly distinguish themselves as subjects of mental phenomena, from all external causes, or objects of the same. They may not be able technically to express this distinction with the clearness and definiteness that a philosopher would. They may not be able to understand, at first, the meaning of the terms he would employ to express that distinction. Still it is, to them, a no less palpable reality, than to him.

As to Consciousness, which is thus seen to be, "in all men, a natural process," "some," in the language of the philosopher above named, "elevate this natural process to the degree of an art, a method, by reflection, which is a sort of second consciousness,—a free re-production of the first, and as consciousness gives all men an idea of what is passing in them, so reflection gives the philosopher a certain knowledge of everything which falls under the eye of consciousness." Reflection, or Philosophic Consciousness, is simple or natural consciousness directed by the will, in the act of careful attention to the phenomena of our minds. As natural consciousness is one of the characteristics, which distinguishes man from the brute, so philosophic consciousness is the characteristics which distinguishes the mental philosopher from the rest of mankind. The above remarks may be illustrated by a reference to two common forms of observation in respect to external, material substances. The phenomena of such substances all mankind alike notice, and to some degree reason about. It is the natural philosopher, however, who attentively observes these phenomena, for the purpose of marking their fundamental characteristics, as the basis of philosophic classification, generalization, etc. The same holds true in respect to the two forms of consciousness under consideration. Mental phenomena all men are conscious of, and all men, to a greater or less degree, are accustomed to reason about. The philosopher, however, by laborious efforts of self-reflection, most critically attends to these phenomena, for the purpose of marking their characteristics, classifying and arranging them according to philosophic principles, and thus determining the powers and laws of mental operations. In simple consciousness, in short we have a knowledge of whatever passes in our minds. In reflection we have the same phenomena classified and generalized, according to fundamental characteristics.

CONSCIOUSNESS A DISTINCT FACULTY OF THE MIND.

Is consciousness a distinct and separate faculty of the mind? On this question, philosophers are not yet fully agreed, and high authority may be cited in support of each side. Sir William Hamilton is commonly reckoned as advocating the negative side of this question. Consciousness as he has defined the subject, he has fully proved not to be such a faculty; and self-consciousness, however, he has defined, and treated as such a faculty: and self-consciousness as defined by him, is, as we have already shown, perfectly identical with consciousness as we have defined the term, and as it is commonly defined by philosophers. The authority of this author therefore, is, in fact, wholly in favor of the doctrine maintained in this treatise, to wit, that consciousness, or self-consciousness, as he has defined the term, is a distinct and separate faculty of the mind. That this is the true theory, we argue from the following considerations:

TRUE THEORY VERIFIED.

1. The intuitive convictions of the race—of all mankind in common, clearly evince the existence in the mind of two distinct and separate forms of knowledge, to wit, that which pertains to external, material substances on the one hand, and that which pertains to the mind itself, on the other. Equally familiar are all men with the two special faculties through which these diverse forms of knowledge are obtained. Nor do they ever confound these forms of knowledge, nor the faculties referred to, the one with the other.

2. Among all civilized nations, this faculty is represented and designated by an appropriate and specific term, a term which is never applied to any other faculty. No term in the English language, for example, has a more fixed, definite, and exclusive, meaning and use than the term Consciousness. No individual misapprehends the meaning of the term, nor misapplies it whenever it is employed: a fact which most clearly evinces how distinctly marked and recognized, this faculty, together with its appropriate objects, is in universal thought.

3. Knowledge by consciousness does, in fact exist in the mind —knowledge, wholly distinct and separate from all other kinds of mental phenomena there found. This is undeniable and is, in fact, universally admitted. To deny to consciousness, therefore, the prerogatives of a distinct and separate faculty of the mind, is to violate all valid and admitted laws of mental classification and deduction.

4. Even those philosophers who deny to this faculty such a prerogative, speak of it, and elucidate it as such a faculty. To this statement we know of no exceptions. The translator of Cousin, for example, after assigning to this faculty the same functions that we have done; after affirming that it is not "a distinct and special faculty," or "a principle of any of the faculties" or "the product of these," thus defines this same thing which he affirms to have no being at all: "Consciousness is a *witness* of our thoughts and volitions."

Precisely similar contradictions appear in the writings and discourses of all who deny the doctrine of this treatise upon this subject.

OBJECTS OF CONSCIOUSNESS CHRONOLOGICALLY ANTECEDENT TO THE CONSCIOUSNESS OF THE SAME.

Perception, in all its forms external and internal, implies, of course, the prior existence of its object, whatever that object may be. Pain, for example, as a state of the sensibility does not exist because we are conscious of it, but we are conscious of it because it does exist; the existence of the object being chronologically antecedent to the consciousness of its existence. The same, does, and must, hold true universally.

CHAPTER IV.

SENSE.

Sense, or the faculty of External Perception, has been defined, as that faculty, or function, of the intelligence, by which we apprehend the phenomena, or qualities of external, material substances.

TO BE DISTINGUISHED FROM SENSATION.

The exercise of this faculty should be carefully distinguished from those states of the Sensibility which always accompany it, but which are, notwithstanding, none the less, for that reason, distinct from it, to wit, sensations. Sensation is the state of the *sensibility* which immediately succeeds any impression made by any cause, upon our physical organization. Sensation is exclusively a state of the sensibility. Sense is no less exclusively a function of the intelligence. Of these distinctions we should never lose sight, when reasoning upon this department of mental science.

SPONTANEOUS AND VOLUNTARY DETERMINATION OF SENSE.

Sense, like consciousness, is, in its primitive developments, a simple spontaneity of the intelligence. Its action, in this state, is, in no sense, conditioned on the will. Perception, in its distinct forms, is conditioned on attention, which is nothing but the perceptive faculty, directed by the will; and hence, for the want of a better term or phrase, called voluntary determination of the faculty. Attention, in the direction of consciousness,—that is, when directed to mental phenomena, is called *reflection.* When in the direction of the faculty of external perception,—that is, towards the phenomena of material substances,—it is called *observation.*

The necessity of observation, that is, of attention, in the voluntary direction of the perceptive faculty towards phenomena obscurely given in the spontaneous developments of that faculty, may be readily illustrated. A portion of a congregation, for example, who have been listening to a certain speaker, have fallen into a state of slumber. The speaker suddenly stops, and immediately all are aroused. Now, if the audience had not, in some form, heard the voice which broke upon their ears, why were they aroused? Yet, if inquired of in respect to what had been spoken to them, they would, for the obvious and exclusive reason that they had not attended to it, be wholly unable to answer. How often do we hear the remark, I gained no distinct conception of that part of a discourse. My attention happened, at the time, to be directed to something else.

The attention may, in some instances, be so fixed upon some object in one direction, that the sensibility and intelligence both may be almost, if not quite, totally isolated from what would otherwise deeply affect us in another direction. A gentleman, for example, who was employed about the machinery in a factory, had one of his fingers entirely cut off, by the sudden and unexpected starting of a portion of that machinery which carried, with great velocity, a circular saw. So intensely did his attention instantly become occupied with the prevention of the destruction of the whole machinery, that he was not aware of the injury done to his own person, nor was he sensible of the least pain from it, till the accident was pointed out to him by another who stood by. As soon, however, as the injury was discovered, the pain from it became intense.

The *basis* of attention is the spontaneous action of the sensibility and intelligence,—action which always occurs, when the proper conditions are fulfilled, and when the mind is not isolated from objects in other directions, by its intense action upon some object (as in the case above cited), in some specific direction.

ORGANS OF SENSE, AND THE KNOWLEDGE CONVEYED BY EACH.

In regard to the particular organs of sense, of which five are commonly reckoned, to wit, sight, hearing, taste, smell, and touch, —organs through which a knowledge, of the particular qualities of material substances is conveyed to the mind, but little need be said. One remark, however, may be deemed of some importance. It is this: each organ pertains exclusively to the particular quality or qualities which are the objects of that particular organ. The peculiar qualities given by sight, for example, are given by no other sense. The *relation* of objects, such as distance, which is a mere relation, and not a quality at all, we learn, by experience, to determine by various senses, as sight, touch, hearing, and smelling even in some instances. But the *existence* and *qualities* of such objects are given, as causes and objects of particular sensations and perceptions in us, by each of the senses alike; each sense, or each organ of the general faculty giving the quality, or qualities, which are the objects of that particular organ.

OBJECTS OF PERCEPTION.

The objects of perception (external perception) are the *qualities* of material substances. The qualities perceived are resistance, extension, form, color, taste, smell, sound, etc. Such qualities are to us the index, and the only index we have, of their respective subjects. In the consciousness of thought, feeling, and mental determinations, we know ourselves as thinking, feeling, and acting beings. So in the experience of sensations and perceptions pro-duced in us by external material substances, we know them as the powers which produce these perceptions and sensations; in other words, we know them as substances possessed of the qualities of resistance, extension, form, color, etc.

THE PROVINCE OF PHILOSOPHY.

Philosophy, it should be borne in mind, has to do with facts as they are, with the nature of the powers revealed in those facts, and with the laws in conformity to which those powers, act. With the mode of their action further than this, it has nothing to do. In the fall of heavy bodies to the earth, for example, we learn that attraction is a property of all material substances. We then set ourselves to determine the law which controls the action of this property. Here we are within the legitimate domain of philosophy. But suppose we attempt to explain the *mode* in which the attractive power acts. "Such knowledge is to wonderful for us. It is high, we cannot attain unto it." Philosophy, well satisfied with her own legitimate and wide domain, resigns such things to the Eternal One, who created all the powers of the universe, and consequently understands the mode of their action. All that philosophy can say in regard to the mode of action of any power is, that such is its nature.

COMPARATIVE VALIDITY OF THE AFFIRMATIONS OF SENSE AND CONSCIOUSNESS.

We are now prepared to contemplate the comparative validity of the affirmations of these two functions of the intelligence, sense and consciousness. I will suppose that I have a perception of some external object, as possessed of the qualities of extension, form, and color. In consciousness I recognize the existence of this perception as a phenomenon of my own mind. Which of these affirmations are, in reality, the most valid, and which would a wise and sound philosophy impel me to esteem and treat as such;—the affirmation of sense, in respect to the qualities of the external object, or of consciousness, in regard to the existence and character of the affirmation of the former faculty, as a phenomenon of the mind itself? Neither, surely. Each faculty pertains alike to its object, by direct and immediate intuition. The affirmation of each is alike positive and absolute in respect to its object. The action of one is, in reality, no more a mystery than that of the other. The *quo modo* of the action of each is alike inexplicable, and no more inexplicable than the mode of action of every other power in existence. It is a sage remark of Dr. Brown, when speaking of the mode in which causes produce their respective effects, "that *everything* is mysterious, or nothing is." When philosophy leads us to doubt the real affirmations of any faculty of the intelligence, then philosophy itself becomes impossible, and the attempt to realize it, the perfection of absurdity.

THEORY OF EXTERNAL PERCEPTION.

The way is now prepared for an enunciation of the theory of external perception, taught in this treatise. Knowledge implies two things; an *object* to be known, and a *subject* capable of knowing. Between the nature of the subject and object there must be such a mutual correlation, that, when certain conditions are fulfilled, knowledge arises, as a necessary result of this correlation. Between matter and mind this correlation exists. The latter knows the former, because the one is a *faculty,* and the other an *object* of knowledge. Mind perceives the qualities of matter, because the former has the *power* of perception, and the latter is an *object* of perception.

Mind also exists in a tri-unity, consisting, as we have seen, of the intelligence, sensibility, and will. To each of these departments of our nature, the external world is correlated. Certain conditions being fulfilled, particular qualities of material substances become to the intelligence, direct objects of knowledge. Other conditions being fulfilled, they affect our sensibility; producing in us certain sensations either pleasurable, painful, or indifferent. Our will then acts upon these substances, controlling their movements, and modifying their states; while they, in turn, react upon the will, modifying and limiting its control. In the first instance, knowledge is direct and immediate. In the second, through a consciousness of sensation, we learn the correlation between those objects and our sensibility. In the last, through a consciousness of the exercise of our will, and an experience of the results, we learn the correlation between these substances and our voluntary powers. In all instances, however, whether our knowledge is direct or indirect, it is alike real and absolute. In respect to the *manner* in which, when certain conditions are fulfilled, we know these objects, the only answer that philosophy gives or demands, is this: Such is the correlation between the nature of the knowing faculty and that of the objects of knowledge.

THEORY VERIFIED.

It is a sufficient verification of the theory above announced, that it is a statement of the case, as it presents itself to the universal intelligence,—that it is encumbered with no difficulties which are not involved in every theory of a different kind which has hitherto been presented, and is entirely free from those difficulties which are perfectly fatal to those theories. Every individual believes, that he knows the external world as correlated to the three departments of our nature under consideration, and in accordance with the principles above stated. Every theory also must rest, in the last analysis, in respect to the *mode of* knowledge, upon this one principle; *The mind knows, because it is a faculty of knowledge.* The difficulties which all theories, contradictory to that above announced, involve, are these: either they do not present the facts or conditions of knowledge, or the manner of knowing, as they are given in and by the universal intelligence.

QUALITIES OF MATTER.

We next direct special attention to consideration of the qualities of matter. According to Sir William Hamilton, and in his classification we fully concur, such qualities may, and according to a strictly scientific arrangement, should, be classed as, primary proper, secundo-primary, and secondary.

PRIMARY QUALITIES.

The first, the primary proper, includes all those properties which belong to matter as such, and which cannot, even in thought, be separated from it, as matter. The necessary constituent elements of our idea of matter, as such, are two,—that it occupies space, and is contained in space; that is, has real extension, solidity and form. Hence, in the language of the author referred to, "we have eight proximate attributes:

1st. Extension,
2nd. Divisibility,
3rd. Size,
4th. Density or Rarity,
5th. Figure (or form),
6th. Incompressibility,
7th. Mobility,
8th. Situation."

These qualities distinguish no one kind of material substance from any other, but matter itself from every other substance; and cannot, even in thought, be separated from it, as matter.

SECUNDO-PRIMARY QUALITIES.

The secundo primary qualities are those which pertain, not to matter, as such, but which distinguish different classes of material substances from one another, and which pertain, as essential qualities, to such classes. Thus bodies in the language of the author quoted from are classed, in reference to their "gravity and cohesion; also as heavy and light, as hard and soft,—solid and fluid,—viscid and friable,—tough and brittle,—rigid and flexible,—fissile and infissile,—ductile and inductile,—elastic and inelastic,—rough and smooth,—slippery and tenacious-compressible and incompressible,—resilient and irresilient,—movable and immovable."

SECONDARY QUALITIES.

The secondary qualities are, properly speaking, Subjective affections in ourselves, and not properties of matter at all. They pertain to matter merely as causes, unperceived in themselves, of these affections or sensations. Such for example, are the qualities represented by the terms: sound, flavor, savor, and actual sensation, heat, cold, etc.

REPRESENTATIVE AND PRESENTATIVE KNOWLEDGE.

Every one is accustomed to distinguish between that kind of knowledge which is *direct* and *immediate,* and that which is obtained *mediately;* that is, through something differing numerically from the *object* of knowledge. The former kind, Sir William Hamilton denominates *presentative,* and the latter, *representative* knowledge. The general faculty of presentative knowledge, he designated by the term consciousness. Whenever we have a direct and immediate perception of an object, we are, he affirms, *conscious* of that object. This general faculty has, he further teaches, two distinct and separate functions—those of external and internal perception; that is, sense, and self-consciousness. In our judgment, we repeat what I have before said; it would be well for science, that these terms, to wit, consciousness, sense, or "the faculty of eternal perception or perception simply," and self-consciousness, were generally employed in strict accordance with the definitions of this author. The term *consciousness* we shall employ as he does; that is, when we wish to affirm that we have a direct and immediate knowledge, perception, of an object, we shall affirm, that we are *conscious,* or are *directly* and *immediately* conscious of that object.

RELATIONS OF THE INTELLIGENCE TO THE QUALITIES OF MATTER.

We are now prepared for a distinct statement of the actual relations of the universal intelligence to the qualities of matter. They are these: Of the primary qualities throughout, and of the secundo-primary in part, to say the least, our knowledge is *direct* and *immediate,* that is, presentative. We are, for example, in external perception, just as directly, immediately, and absolutely conscious of matter as an external object actually possessed of the qualities of *extension and form,* as we are, in internal perception, of ourselves, as exercising the functions of thought, feeling, and willing. It would be no more an impeachment of the absolute testimony of universal consciousness to deny one of the above propositions, than it would be to deny the other. Our knowledge of the secondary qualities of this substance, on the other hand, is wholly representative; that is, indirect and mediate, being obtained wholly through the consciousness of our varied sensations. The secondary qualities are given in the universal consciousness, as the *unknown causes* of *conscious states* of the *sensibility, sensations.* The primary, and secundo-primary, on the other hand, are as universally given in consciousness, as the *known objects* of *conscious* states of the *intelligence.* Here is found the fundamental distinction in the relations of the universal intelligence to the different qualities of matter.

FUNDAMENTAL ERROR IN PHILOSOPHY.

By many philosophers, the dogma is maintained, that *all* our knowledge of matter is exclusively representative, being indirectly and mediately derived, through sensation. We might, with the same truth and propriety, affirm that we have *no* knowledge of this substance, through this medium, as to affirm that *all* our knowledge of it is thus derived. We should no more deny conscious facts, to affirm that *all* our knowledge of matter is presentative, than we should to affirm, as the sensational theory does, that all our knowledge of it is representative. We are, as we have said, directly and immediately conscious of matter, as far as its primary qualities are concerned, as the known object of known acts of the intelligence, sense, perception; and unless universal consciousness is "a liar from the beginning," presentative is the only form of knowledge of which these qualities are the objects. We are conscious of the secondary qualities, on the other hand, but in this one form exclusively, as the *unknown causes* of conscious states of the sensibility, sensations; and this is the only sense and form in which our knowledge of matter is received through this one medium. The sensational theory has no other foundation than a partial induction of the facts of consciousness, being compatible with one part, and absolutely incompatible with the other:

HAS MATTER A REAL OR ONLY AN IDEAL EXISTENCE?

Till quite recently, a fundamental difficulty has attended the discussion of this question; the almost universally admitted assumption, that all our knowledge of this substance is exclusively representative, being derived wholly through the medium of sensation. While that assumption remained as an admitted principle in the science of mind, it was absolutely impossible to vindicate for matter anything more than an ideal existence; that of an unknown, and unknowable cause of a given mental state, sensation. As the existence of this state could be accounted for equally well, on various and opposite hypotheses, no positive evidence of an external, material cause could, by any possibility, be adduced. Now, however, the sensational theory has been demonstrably exploded, within the sphere of science. It has been demonstrably established, that *all* our knowledge of this substance is not through the medium of sensation; that all our knowledge of its primary qualities, to say the least, is, not mediate or representative, but direct and immediate, or presentative. "In our perception consciousness" says Sir William Hamilton, "there is revealed as an ultimate fact, a *self* and a *not-self*—each given as independent, each known only in antithesis to the other. No belief is more *intuitive,*

63

universal, immediate, or *irresistible,* than that this antithesis is real and known to be real; no belief is therefore more true. If the antithesis be illusive—*self* and *not-self, subject* and *object,* and *Thou,* are distinctions without a difference; and consciousness, so far from being "the internal voice of our Creator" is shown to be like Satan, "a liar from the beginning." Matter, then, as a substance external to the mind, and possessed of the properties of resistance, extension, and form, has *real* being.

THE DOCTRINE OF MATTER AS A FORCE VOID OF THE PRIMARY QUALITIES, SUCH AS SOLIDITY, EXTENSION AND FORM.

The doctrine is how being pressed with great zeal into the sphere of science, that matter is, not an extended substance having resistance and form, but an indefinable and inconceivable something, denominated a force. This has become the watchword of a new school in philosophy, to wit: Matter has real existence, not however, as a material substance having real resistance, extension, and form, but as an immaterial something, acting in space as a force. Let us contemplate this new doctrine for a few moments.

Those who agree with us have no controversy with this school in regard to the question, whether matter is, in its nature, a real force. This is the common doctrine of all schools who believe in an external world. What we contend for is this; that the idea of matter as a force, is just as compatible with the doctrine, that it has the properties of real resistance, extension, and form, as with the dogma, that it has no such properties. We further contend, that the advocates of the new doctrine have never yet developed a solitary fact pertaining to the nature of the forces operating in the universe around us, that proves, or renders it, in the remotest degree, probable that matter does not, in fact, possess the qualities under consideration, together with all primary, and secundo-primary qualities which have been attributed to it. We contend still further, that from an appeal to the nature of the case, it cannot be shown, that the remotest *antecedent* probability exists in favor of this new doctrine, and against that which we maintain. In itself, it is just as conceivable, just as possible, and just as probable, that the forces existing and operating, in space, and occupying space, have, for example the qualities of real resistance, extension, and form, as that they have no such qualities. We finally adduce against this new doctrine, and in favor of the one which we maintain, the absolute affirmations of the universal consciousness. Either that consciousness is a lie, or we have absolute knowledge of the forms existing and operating in, and occupying space, as possessed of the qualities under consideration. The whole subject before us stands thus:

1. This new doctrine is not self-evidently true. This, no one will deny.

2. It cannot, by any possibility, be proved to be true. This is equally undeniable.

3. Not a solitary real fact can be adduced which renders its truth, in the remotest degree, probable.

4. It has not a single element of *antecedent* probability in its favor.

5. This new doctrine is confronted, and the opposite doctrine affirmed as true, by the direct, immediate, and absolute affirmations of the universal consciousness. Either knowledge is not knowledge, that is, it is not it, or this new doctrine is false, and the one we maintain is true; the former having no other foundation than mere assumptions based upon infinite ignorance, while the latter is based upon the immovable rock of truth, absolute knowledge. We may safely challenge the advocates of the new doctrine to present a solitary real fact, or a valid argument, in any form, that invalidates or weakens the force of any of the propositions above presented.

IS COLOR A PRIMARY, OR A SECONDARY QUALITY OF MATTER?

In all schools of philosophy, known to us, color is assumed to be merely a secondary quality of matter. Into this error Sir William Hamilton has fallen, although he has himself given, with perfect correctness, the distinguishing characteristic which separates the primary from the secondary quality, and, in express words, and with equal correctness, has given this identical characteristic to this one quality, color. The primary quality, he tells us, cannot, even in thought, be separated from matter, but necessarily pertains to it as such a substance. He then gives forth the following statement in regard to the quality under consideration,—a statement the validity of which will not be questioned: "As Aristotle has observed, we cannot imagine body without *all* color, though we can imagine it without *any one.*" Color, then, is a primary quality of matter, or this substance has no such qualities at all. The particular colors by which different objects are distinguished from one another, constitute the secundo-primary qualities of matter. For a more full and complete discussion of the true doctrine of sense, or external perception, we would refer to the chapter on this subject in the larger work, the Intellectual Philosophy.

CHAPTER V.

REASON.

Reason has already been defined, as the faculty of *implied knowledge,* the faculty which gives us necessary ideas,—ideas necessarily implied by the facts perceived, and apprehended by the faculties of external and internal perception, sense, and consciousness. Through sense,—perception, for example, we have a direct and immediate consciousness of body, as possessed of the qualities of extension and form. By reason, on occasion of such perceptions, we apprehend space, in which body does and must exist, the former being implied by the latter; that is, the existence of body being absolutely impossible, but upon the condition that space in which the former exists, and which it occupies, does exist. In the consciousness of external and internal facts, occurring as they do, one after the other, we obtain the idea of succession; and by reason, on occasion of such apprehension, we cognize time, or duration, as necessarily *implied by* succession. By sense and consciousness, also, we perceive phenomena. On occasion of such perceptions and as necessarily implied by the same, reason cognizes substance. By external and internal perception, too, we apprehend events. By reason, on occasion of such apprehensions, we cognize cause as necessarily implied by events. Of body and succession we are conscious as limited, and of space and duration, as unlimited. On occasion of the consciousness of such attributes in these objects, reason apprehends the correlative ideas of the finite, on the one hand, and of the infinite, on the other. On occasion of the consciousness of ourselves as the subjects of internal phenomena, reason apprehends the idea of personal identity, as necessarily implied by such conscious facts. On the perception of any fact external or internal, reason apprehends still another idea, that of *existence,* an idea represented by the verb to be, in its various forms. So also on the perception of various objects, reason apprehends the ideas of resemblance and difference, likeness and unlikeness, equality and inequality, unity and plurality, or number, etc.

Reason being exclusively the faculty of implied knowledge, its sphere is thus fixed, determined, and limited. Its action is always conditioned on the prior action of the other faculties, and the essential characteristics of all truths attained by reason, must be as are those of the facts and objects known as real, through these faculties. From the nature of the case, this must be so. Implied knowledge must, in its essential characteristics, be determined by that by which the former is implied. Space and time, for example, are known, and can be conceived of, but as the place of body and succession, and all our ideas of substances and causes existing and operating in time and space, must be as is our knowledge of the particular phenomena and effects attributed to said substances and causes. The exclusive sphere of reason, we repeat, is to *apprehend* the *realities directly* and *immediately implied,* and *necessarily so, by the facts and objects known and affirmed as real by and through the other primary faculties.*

PRIMARY AND SECONDARY IDEAS OF REASON.

Reason, as we have shown, gives us apprehensions of realities implied as real by facts and objects affirmed as such by the other intellectual faculties. In connection with the action of the primary faculties, sense and consciousness, it apprehends such realities as space, time, the finite and the infinite, substance, personal identity, and cause. In connection with the action of the secondary faculties, to be elucidated hereafter, it apprehends other realities implied as such by objects given as real through these faculties. Those ideas of reason attained through the action of the primary faculties; as, the ideas of space, time, the finite and the infinite, substance, personal identity, and cause, we denominate the primary ideas of reason. Those on the other hand, attained through the action of the secondary faculties; such for example, as the ideas of God, duty, the true, the beautiful, the good, liberty, necessity, immortality, and retribution, we denominate the secondary ideas of reason. The former class of ideas enter, as elements, into all our conceptions of objects of every kind. The latter constitute the laws of thought and action in all their forms. The former have been already sufficiently elucidated in this and the preceding chapters; the latter will be elucidated in a separate chapter, after we shall have developed the nature and characteristics of the secondary faculties referred to.

VALIDITY OF KNOWLEDGE BY REASON.

Implied knowledge has the same validity and can have no more than the knowledge by which the former is implied has. Knowledge, through sense and consciousness, has, as we have seen, absolute validity for the reality and character of its objects. Knowledge by reason, therefore, has the same validity. Body, succession, phenomena external and internal, and events, have, not an *ideal,* but a *real,* and *actually known* existence, and are, in themselves, as apprehended by the intelligence. Space, time, substance, personal identity, and cause, are in themselves, and to the mind, actually known realities. Materialism, idealism, and skepticism,—all of which rest wholly upon this one assumption announced by Kant, that we do not, and cannot know realities as they are in themselves; that the objects of all our ideas and conceptions are "not in themselves what we take them to be," are systems of "science falsely so called." Materialism impeaches the validity of our knowledge of mind. Idealism impeaches the validity of that of matter, and both systems that of all implied knowledge. Skepticism, in the language of the author just named, "gives out all things as mere *appearance,"* denying the validity of knowledge in all its forms alike. We have seen, that our knowledge through all the primary faculties is valid for realities, as they are in themselves. In reasoning from facts to principles, from the finite to the infinite, from creation to a personal God, for example, we are not reasoning from the unknown to the still more profoundly unknown, but from the absolutely known to the necessarily implied. The student in mental science cannot be too deeply impressed with the fact, that right here lies the only real issue between theism and anti-theism. The latter affirms that, in our reasonings from assumed facts to final causes, we are, in truth, reasoning from the absolutely unknown to the still more profoundly unknown. The former affirms that, in thus reasoning, we are, in fact, advancing through the absolutely known to the necessarily implied. The deductions of each system have an immutably necessary connection with its principles, and must stand or fall with said principles. We either do, or do not, know the essential facts of nature, and do, or do not, know them as they are in themselves. If we do thus know these facts, then all schools in science admit and affirm that the doctrine of the being and perfections of a personal God is based upon eternal rock, the rock of truth. If on the other hand, as anti-theism affirms, we do not thus know these facts; if nature is to us absolutely unknown and unknowable,—then it is infinite folly in us to inquire at all after ultimate causes in any form; that is, to attempt to deduce, from infinite ignorance, absolute knowledge.

FUNDAMENTAL MISTAKE IN REGARD TO THE SPHERE AND FUNCTIONS OF KNOWLEDGE A PRIORI.

Knowledge through reason, has been denominated by some philosophers, knowledge *a priori*, and many and very wild speculations have been indulged in, respecting the proper sphere and functions of such knowledge. Among these speculations, the two following deserve special attention.

ERROR OF THE GERMAN PHILOSOPHERS.

By direct insight of reason, or by knowledge *a priori*, the German philosophers, since the time of Kant, professedly determine the validity of knowledge by means of all the other intellectual faculties, and even by reason itself. On the assumed authority of such insight, they have pronounced all knowledge existing in the mind, even ideas of reason, utterly invalid.

"We have therefore intended to say," says Kant, in giving the results of his philosophy, "that all our intuition is nothing but the representation of phenomenon—that the things which we envisage (form conceptions and judgments of) are not that in themselves for which we take them; neither are their relationships in themselves so constituted as they appear to us; and that if we do away with our subject, or even only the subjective quality of the senses in general, every quality, all relationships of objects in space and time, nay, even space and time themselves would disappear, and cannot exist as phenomena in themselves, but only in us. It remains utterly unknown to us what may be the nature of the objects in themselves, separate from all the receptivity of our sensibility. We know nothing but our manner of perceiving them, which is peculiar to us, and which need not belong to every being, although to every man.

"With this only we have to do." With this assumption, all the German philosophers since the time of Kant fully agree. Now it is utterly impossible to conceive of a greater absurdity, or of forms of more palpable self-contradiction, in the sphere of philosophy, than is involved in the above doctrine in respect to the proper functions of reason, or of knowledge *a priori*. What authority has implied knowledge to determine the validity of that by which it is implied? In other words, how can a faculty, whose exclusive province is to apprehend realities implied, and only known as implied by facts and objects affirmed as real by other distinct and separate faculties, determine the validity of the affirmations of said faculties? How can any faculty determine the validity of its own absolute affirmations? How, for example, can intuition determine the validity of knowledge by intuition, and how can vision itself determine the validity of knowledge by vision? Finally, how can we, through faculties known to deceive us utterly everywhere else, obtain valid knowledge of "our manner of perceiving objects?" The whole German philosophy has its exclusive basis in mere assumptions,— assumptions involving the most palpable absurdities and contradictions of which we can possibly form a conception.

ERROR OF PRESIDENT HICKOK AND OTHERS.

President Hickok, together with a school of philosophy of which he is the most distinguished representative, claims for reason, or knowledge *a priori,* a still higher and more far-reaching insight. By such insight, first of all, he professedly determined, in harmony with the teachings of the transcendental philosophy of Germany, that our perceptive faculties, sense and consciousness, do not cognize facts and objects in the world of matter and spirit, as they are; that no objects exist in space, objects having real extension and form, such as are absolutely affirmed to exist by the universal consciousness; but that space, on the other hand, is occupied by mere forces utterly void of the attributes named above. On the authority of the same insight, he affirms that we can obtain, through nature, no valid proof of the being and perfections of God, but that the infinite is cognized as real by direct and immediate insight of reason. Thus, on the authority of knowledge *a priori,* correcting inspiration in the assertion, that "the invisible things of Him (God) from the creation of the world *are clearly seen,* being understood," not by direct insight or reason, but *"by the things that are made,* even His eternal power and God head." In his rational cosmology, he professedly determines purely and exclusively by knowledge *a priori,* not only the nature of the forces existing and acting in the world around us, but the precise mode in which these forces were created and organized. In short, by direct insight of reason, or *by knowledge a priori,* he professedly gives not only the nature of space and time, but of all the substances, forces, and causes,—finite and infinite, existing and acting in time and space.

Now the merest tyro in philosophy ought to know, that reason, or knowledge *a priori,* has, and can have, no such insight, sphere, or authority as is here assigned to it. Independent of, and prior to the action of the perceptive faculties, it has, in reality, no insight at all; and when it does act, it can do no more nor less than give the realities *implied* as such by facts and objects affirmed as real by these faculties. Within this sphere, and nowhere else, has it authority, and here its authority is absolute, just as is the authority of each of the perceptive faculties within its proper sphere, and in respect to its appropriate objects. In respect to the question, what substances or causes do exist, reason has no direct and immediate insight at all. Let us contemplate this subject in still another point of light. Of two or more distinct and opposite hypotheses each of which is, with each and every other, equally conceivable, and as a consequence, equally possible, we cannot determine *a priori* which is, and which is not, true. This is undeniable. Of two events, for example, each of which is in itself as possible, and as likely to happen, as the other, we cannot determine *a priori* which will happen. Now when we contemplate time and space by themselves, three distinct and separate hypotheses present themselves in respect to what events and substances finite and infinite, do occur and exist in time and space, to wit:

1. No events do occur in time, and no substances do exist in space.

2. Events do occur and substances do exist in time and space; but neither are to us objects of valid knowledge.

3. Events do occur in time, and substances do exist in space, and both are to the mind objects of valid knowledge. How can we determine *a priori* which of these hypotheses is, and which is not, true? How can reason, the faculty of implied knowledge, and that only, look into empty time and space, and, by direct and immediate and independent insight, determine whether any, and if so, what events do occur in time, and what substances, forces, and causes finite and infinite, do exist and act in space. No hypotheses can be more self-evidently absurd and false, than is the *idea,* that reason has such insight, or that knowledge *a priori* has any such authority as is ascribed to it by this author and his school in philosophy.

CHAPTER VI.

SECONDARY FACULTIES.

UNDERSTANDING DEFINED.

Through the faculty of sense, and a consciousness of sensations, we have, as we have seen, intuitions of the qualities of external material substances; phenomena, such as are expressed by the terms extension, form, resistance, color, taste, smell, and sound. By consciousness, we have similar intuitions of the operations of our minds; such as thinking, feeling, and willing. Through reason, on condition of the perceptions of sense and consciousness, we have intuitions such as those of time, space, personal identity, substance, and cause. These intuitions being given, another and secondary intellectual process occurs, a process in which said intuitions, necessary and contingent, are united into *notions,* or conceptions of particular things. Thus, our notion of body, for example, is complex, and when analyzed into its distinct elements, is found to be constituted exclusively of intuitions given by the faculties above referred to. We conceive of it as a substance, in which the qualities named inhere,—a substance existing in time and space, and sustaining certain relations to other substances, of which we have notions similarly compounded. The same holds true of our notions of all substances whatever. They are all complex, and constituted exclusively of intuitions given by the primary faculties. *A notion, then, is a complex intellectual phenomenon, composed of intuitions.*

The faculties, or functions of the intelligence, which give us the latter, we have already considered. What shall we call that which gives us the former? In other words, what shall we call the *notion-forming* power of the mind? In conformity to a usage which has, since the time of Coleridge, extensively obtained, we denominate this faculty of the intelligence, the understanding. In strict conformity to this specific application, will the term understanding, when special notice to the contrary is not given, be employed

74

throughout this treatise. It will be employed, not as Locke uses it, as designating the general intelligence, but as a function in which intuitions, contingent and necessary, given by the primary faculties, are combined, into *notions or conceptions of particular objects, or classes of objects.*

SOURCE OF ERROR.

As intuition, in all instances, pertains directly, immediately and singly, to its object, intuitive perception must be held as always valid for the reality and character of its object. All forms of scientific procedure have their basis in the assumed truth of this one principle, *the validity of intuition for the reality and character of its object.* Error, on the other hand, commences with conceptions, or notions. How often do we hear one individual say to another: your *"conception* of such and such object, is right or wrong, true or false."* How often are grave conclusions, and trains of reasoning, based upon misapprehensions of the subject to which such conclusions and reasoning pertain. The disciple of truth will be exceeding careful in the formation of conceptions in respect to all important objects of thought.

NOTIONS, OR CONCEPTIONS, CLASSIFIED.

We are now prepared for a distinct classification of these intellectual apprehensions, phenomena which take rank under different, and varied classes, according to the point of light in which they are, from time to time, contemplated.

VALID AND INVALID CONCEPTIONS.

One of the most obvious divisions is that of valid and invalid, or true and false. A conception or notion is valid for the reality and character of its object, that is, is true, when it *embraces the perceived and implied elements of thought actually given by intuition in respect to its object.* It is invalid or false, when it *excludes any elements thus given,* or *includes any not thus given.* This is the universal criterion of valid and invalid, true and false, conceptions.

COMPLETE AND INCOMPLETE CONCEPTIONS.

A conception or notion is complete when it embraces fully all the attributes of its object. A conception is incomplete, when it embraces but a part of such attributes. A conception, though incomplete, is true or valid, when it embraces none but real attributes. It is false, though complete, when it includes attributes not real, or excludes those which are real.

SPONTANEOUS AND REFLECTIVE CONCEPTIONS.

There are two distinct and opposite states in which a given conception may be contemplated, to wit, as it first appears in consciousness through the spontaneous and primitive action of the understanding; and as it appears when each element embraced in it has been the object of distinct reflection, and the entire conception, with all its constituent elements, is presented in consciousness in a distinct and reflective form. The former may be classed as spontaneous, and the latter as reflective conceptions; the former being indistinct and undefined, and the latter always appearing in the consciousness in forms distinct and well defined. The importance of habitually forming full, and distinct, or reflective, apprehensions of all important objects of thought, cannot be overestimated. It is worse than useless, for example, to read books, or listen to discourses, unless we habituate ourselves to the formation of distinct, and reflective, apprehensions of what we read or hear.

INDIVIDUAL, GENERIC OR GENERICAL, AND SPECIFIC OR SPECIFICAL CONCEPTIONS.

Conceptions which pertain to single objects, or to individuals, are denominated individual conceptions. Those which pertain to *kinds,* which embrace, not individuals, but classes (species) under them, are denominated generic or generical conceptions. Those, on the other hand, which pertain to the classes (species) referred to, are denominated specific, or specifical conceptions. The species ranks under the genus, and the individual ranks under the species. The individual conception embraces *all* the elements given by intuition in regard to the object of the conception. Specific conceptions embrace only those elements common to all individuals which rank under them. The generical conception embraces only those elements common to all the specifical conceptions which rank under it.

CONCRETE AND ABSOLUTE CONCEPTIONS.

Concrete conceptions pertain to their objects as they actually exist, and embrace all the elements given by intuition, relatively to their objects—conceptions represented by such terms as John, man, animal, etc. Abstract conceptions, on the other hand pertain only to some single quality given by intuition irrespective of the object to which the quality belongs,—conceptions represented by such terms as goodness, whiteness, hardness, etc.

POSITIVE, PRIVATIVE AND NEGATIVE CONCEPTIONS.

Conceptions which embrace those elements only which are actually given by intuition in respect to their objects, are called positive conceptions, such, for example, as are represented by such terms as sound, speech, knowledge, wisdom, etc. Conceptions which pertain to their objects as void of certain qualities which might, but do not, belong to said objects, are denominated privative conceptions, such, for example, as are represented by such terms as dumbness, deafness, ignorance, etc. When, on the other hand a conception pertains to its object as merely, or necessarily, void of certain qualities, it is called a negative conception,—conceptions, for example, represented by such terms as a dumb statue, a lifeless corpse, etc.

CONCRETE AND CHARACTERISTIC CONCEPTIONS.

We commonly have two classes of conceptions in regard to the same class of objects, the one embracing all the elements given by intuition in respect to said objects, and the other comprehending those only which peculiarize and distinguish such objects from all individuals resembling said objects, but belonging to other classes. The former class of conceptions, the concrete, we have already defined. The latter may be denominated characteristic conceptions.

77

INFERIOR AND SUPERIOR CONCEPTIONS.

When our conception takes rank, as an individual, under another as its specifical, or as a specifical under another as its generical conception, the former is denominated the inferior, and the latter the superior, conception.

MISTAKE IN REGARD TO NOTIONS OR CONCEPTIONS.

Conceptions have been sometimes defined as *perceptions recalled.* This is a mistake. Perception may be reproduced, the object being present, but cannot be recalled, the object being absent. Whenever we perceive an object, the understanding forms a notion, or conception, of said object, the perceptive, and notion-forming power often acting instantaneously. In memory, or association, the conception, or notion, formed of the object when perceived is recalled, and not the perception of it.

A FACT OFTEN ATTENDING PERCEPTION.

It is a fact with which all are familiar, that when we unexpectedly meet an object before unknown to us, but which, in certain particulars, resembles one well known, we seem for a time to see the latter with perfect distinctness. The reason of this phenomenon we suppose to be this: under such circumstances, the *notion* we have of the known object is recalled with such vividness, that it almost exclusively occupies the attention of the mind.

MISTAKE OF MR. STEWART.

According to this philosopher, in all conceptions, the absent object is, in the first instance, always believed to be present, as an object of direct perception. Universal consciousness affirms the error of such a dogma. The mistake of Mr. S. arose, as we suppose, from his definition of conception, that is, that it is a past perception recalled. If this were true, we do not see but that we must, not only at first, but at all times, regard the object of our conception, as directly present.

MISTAKE OF COLERIDGE IN RESPECT TO THE UNDERSTANDING.

Coleridge defines the understanding, as the "faculty of judging according to sense," a definition which he copied from Kant and other German philosophers. According to such philosophers, the understanding pertains only to external material substances. It has nothing to do with the subjective, with mind. Now this is a great error in philosophy. As a matter of fact, we form notions and conceptions of mind as really as we do of anything not ourselves. Notions subjective as really exist, in consciousness, as those which are objective. Nor can any reasons be assigned, why we should attribute the formation of the latter to one faculty of the intelligence, and that of the former to another. The appropriate sphere of the understanding is evidently limited only by the finite. Reason alone pertains to the infinite, the absolute, and the universal. All other realities fall within the range of the understanding.

CHAPTER VII.

JUDGMENT.

FACULTY DEFINED.

Through the action of the primary faculties, as we have seen, we obtain the constituent elements of all our knowledge. Through the action of the understanding, as we have also seen, we form *notions,* or *conceptions* particular and general, of varied objects of thought. When such conceptions have been formed, and two or more of them are present in the consciousness, another operation fundamentally distinct from any which we have yet contemplated, occurs; an operation in which a particular *relation* is affirmed to exist between said conceptions, or the subjects of the same. To form a conception of A and B for example, and to judge that A and B agree or disagree with each other, that they resemble or are unlike, that they are equal, or unequal to, each other, are undeniably mental operations entirely distinct and separate, the one from the other. The faculty of conceptions, or the notion-forming power, we have already defined as the understanding. What shall we denominate the faculty to which all "relative suggestions," relative affirmations, or acts of judgment, shall be referred? In accordance with a usage which, to a greater or less extent; has obtained, since the time of Kant, we denominate this new faculty, the judgment. The reality, nature, and sphere, of the faculty of judgment have now been fully ascertained. We will, accordingly, proceed to an elucidation of the leading characteristics of varied acts of this faculty.

ACTS OF JUDGMENT CLASSIFIED.

Acts of judgment take rank in different classes according to the varied standpoints from which they are contemplated. We will consider the following as examples:

QUANTITY OF JUDGMENTS, AS UNIVERSAL, PARTICULAR, AND INDIVIDUAL OR SINGULAR.

In respect to their *quantity,* that is, to the number of individuals to which they pertain, they are classed, as *universal, particular,* and *individual* or singular; as in the case of those represented by the propositions, all men are mortal, some men are mortal, and John is mortal. In the first proposition mortality is affirmed of all individuals represented by the term men. This judgment is, for this reason, denominated *universal.* In the second proposition mortality is affirmed of a part only of the race represented by the term men. Such judgment consequently, is called particular. The last judgment affirms mortality of a single individual, and hence is, denominated a singular or an *individual* judgment. All judgments, when contemplated in reference to the idea of quantity, take rank, as *universal, particular,* or *individual* or *singular,* judgments.

QUALITY OF JUDGMENTS AS AFFIRMATIVE OR NEGATIVE.

As to their quality, judgments are classed as *affirmative,* or *negative;* as in the propositions, all men are mortal, and mind is not matter. In the former case, the predicate is affirmed, and in the latter, it is denied of the subject.

RELATIONS OF JUDGMENTS, AS CATEGORICAL, HYPOTHETICAL AND DISJUNCTIVE.

When our conception is directly affirmed or denied of another as in the propositions, all men are mortal, and mind is not matter, the judgment is denominated *categorical.* When conceptions, in a given judgment, stand related as antecedent and consequent; as in the judgment, "if Caesar was a tyrant, he deserved death," said judgment is denominated *hypothetical.* When one conception is given as included in a single member of a given class; as in the judgment, "Caesar was a hero or a usurper," or it is in B, C, or D, the judgment is said to be *disjunctive.* From the nature of the relation between the subject and predicate in judgments, all such affirmations must be either categorical, hypothetical, or disjunctive.

By Asa Mahan.

MODALITY OF JUDGMENTS AS PROBLEMATICAL, ASSERTATIVE, CONTINGENT AND NECESSARY.

When the connection between the subject and predicate of a given proposition is conceived of as merely possible, that is, with the conviction that the relation designated may, or may not, exist; as in the judgment, A may be in B, the judgment is problematical. When the connection is conceived of, as not only possible, but actual, the judgment affirming such connection as, for example, A is in B, is called *assertative.* When this connection is conceived as actual, with the conviction, that it might possibly be otherwise, as in the proposition, B to-day does exist, as A did yesterday, the judgment is denominated *contingent.* When, on the other hand, a given relation between conceptions or their objects, is considered not only as actual, but attended with the conviction, that the facts of the case, can, by no possibility, be otherwise than they are, the judgment affirming such connection is denominated *necessary* or apodeictical; as in the judgments, body implies space, succession implies time, and events imply a cause.

Contemplated in reference to the idea of modality, all judgments must be classed as *problematical, assertative, contingent* or *necessary.* All contingent and necessary judgments are also assertative.

INTUITIVE AND DEDUCTIVE JUDGMENTS.

All valid judgments may be ranked under one or the other of two classes denominated *intuitive,* or *deductive.* When the validity of a given judgment is directly and immediately discerned; as in the judgments, body implies space, succession implies time, events imply a cause, and things equal to the same thing are equal to one another, the judgment is said to be intuitive. When the validity of a given judgment is evinced, as an inference from other judgments, it is denominated a deduced or deductive judgment.

EMPIRICAL OR EXPERIENCE AND RATIONAL OR A PRIORI JUDGMENTS.

When the validity of a given judgment is evinced by direct and immediate perception external or internal, said judgment is called

82

an *empirical* or *experience* judgment. Two objects in immediate contact, for example, are directly perceived to be equal or unequal. The judgment, affirming their equality or inequality, is denominated an empirical or experience judgment. All judgments pertaining to facts of internal and external perception are of this character. All such judgments, also, are contingent and intuitive.

When, on the other hand, independent of all experience, it is immediately perceived, that from the nature of the relations between the subject and predicate, a given judgment *must* be valid, it is denominated a rational, or *a priori,* that is, a self-evident judgment. Of this character are such judgments as this, every event has a cause. We need no facts of observation or experience, to know that such a judgment *cannot* be invalid. Such judgments have, not only intuitive, but necessary certainty. Hence, in scientific language, they are called *a priori* judgments.

FUNDAMENTAL CHARACTERISTICS OF ALL SUCH JUDGMENTS.

Philosophers, in all ages, have recognized the existence of judgments *a priori,* that is, of judgments possessed of an intuitive and necessary certainty. Yet no philosopher has heretofore attempted even, to give the fundamental characteristics, criteria or tests of such judgments. Such criteria we will now attempt to give. On what conditions, then, can any judgment have intuitive and necessary certainty? We answer, on one or the other of the three following conditions exclusively:

1. The predicate must be identical with, or an essential part of, the subject. When we say, for example, that A is A, we know that the judgment cannot be false; for whatever A may be, it must be equal to, and identical with, itself. Such judgments are called tautological judgments and are, of course, though self-evident, of very little, if of any, use in science. When we say, on the other hand, that all bodies have extension, the predicate, in that case, represents an essential element of the subject, and must, of necessity, pertain to the subject. All judgments, then, in which the predicate represents a known and necessary element of the subject, and is affirmed of it as such, must have intuitive and necessary certainty. Such judgments are called explicative; because the

predicate is explicative of the subject: these are of great use in science.

2. The second class of judgments which have intuitive and necessary certainty, includes those in which the subject implies the predicate; that is, the reality of the object, or the occurrence of the fact, represented by the subject, is necessarily conceived of as impossible but upon the condition of the actual existence of the object or cause represented by the predicate. The judgments to which we have before referred are of this character, to wit, body implies space, succession implies time, phenomena implies substance, and events imply a cause.

On reflection, it will be perceived, at once, that in each of these judgments, the subject implies the predicate. If body, for example, does exist, space must exist. So of succession and time. If succession is real, time must be real. The same holds true of the relations between phenomena and substance, and events and cause. The former cannot be, unless the latter is, real. Such judgments must have necessary intuitive certainty, their contraries being conceived as absolutely impossible. The fundamental principles and axioms in all the sciences are of this character. Judgments of this character are called *implicative* judgments.

3. Where the relation of absolute incompatibility is necessarily conceived as existing between two conceptions, or objects, and the judgment affirms this incompatibility, such judgment also has the character of intuitive and necessary certainty. Of this character are such judgments as these: it is impossible for the same thing at the same time to exist and not to exist; and infinity and perfection cannot err in judgment.

Judgments of this character are called *incompatible* judgments, and must have intuitive and necessary certainty. On reflection, it will be readily apprehended, that all judgments falling under one or the other of the three relations above specified, must have this form of certainty, and that none but such can possess these characteristics. The criteria given by other philosophers, are rather *external* and *circumstantial,* than intrinsically characteristic as all scientific criteria should be. We refer to such criteria as those given by Dr. Ried and others; such for example, as the fact, that all men do admit their validity in all their reasoning; that even those who deny their validity act upon them; and that if they are denied, the validity of all reasoning fails. No such criteria lead the student to consider the nature of the relation between the subject and predicate in such judgment, and reveal to him the fact, that they not only *are,* but *must be, true,* the very ends accomplished by the tests which we have given.

ACTION OF THE JUDGMENT IN THE FORMATION OF ABSTRACT AND GENERAL CONCEPTIONS AND PURE IDEAS OF REASON.

Abstract and general notions or conceptions, and pure ideas of reason, have already been defined. In the primitive developments of the intelligence, no such conceptions or ideas, of course, exist. All then and there is concrete and particular. How are the *general,* the *abstract,* and pure rational ideas, evolved from the concrete and particular?

ABSTRACTION.

All our notions, or understanding conceptions are, as we have seen, complex, constituted, of elements furnished by the primary faculties, sense, consciousness, and reason. To make an abstraction of a notion is, in thought, on the ground of the ideas of resemblance and difference, to separate these elements flow one another, giving special attention to some one, or more, or each of them in particular.

Into our conceptions of body, for example, the elements of form, solidity, color, etc., enter. In the light of the ideas of resemblance and difference, the intelligence perceives at once, that the element of solidity differs from that of form, and that of color from either of the others. In thought, therefore, either of these qualities may be so separated from all the rest that it shall be the object of special reflection, or observation. Thus our conceptions of each quality of the object, and as a consequence, of the object itself, may become more or less distinct and complete. The way is now prepared to answer the inquiry,—how are the conceptions and ideas above referred to formed in the mind?

GENERAL NOTIONS.

In answering this inquiry, we begin with general notions. We will take for example and illustration, the notion designated by the word mountain. It is admitted, that in the first development of the intelligence, there was no such general notion in the mind. The intelligence began not with the general notion, but with the conception of some particular mountain which had before been an object of perception. How then is the general eliminated from the particular? Another mountain becomes an object of perception. Under the influence of the associating principle, the first notion is recalled. The judgment, as these perceptions are present on the theatre of consciousness, separates the elements common to the two. The understanding now combines these common elements into a new conception, under which the judgment subsumes the two particulars. On the perception of a third mountain, the general notion, in a manner like that just described, undergoes a new modification, by which it embraces those elements only, common to the three particulars, while each particular is again classed under the general. Thus the process goes on, till the notion under consideration assumes its most general form. This is the process by which general notions are, in all instances, formed, a process so particularly elucidated in a former chapter, that nothing further need be said upon it here.

ABSTRACT NOTIONS.

We will now consider the origin and genesis of abstract notions such as are designated by such terms as redness, sweetness. These are distinguished from general notions, and also from necessary and universal ideas, by this characteristic. They designate some single quality of particular substances without reference to those substances.

To form general notions, more than one object must be given. To form abstract notions but one is required. Example: This apple is red. When we have separated the quality designated by the term red, from the subject to which it belongs, we then have the abstract notion designated by the term redness. The same holds in all other instances.

UNIVERSAL AND NECESSARY IDEAS.

In explaining the origin and genesis of universal and necessary ideas, in their abstract and universal form, we will take as the basis of our explanation and illustration the principle of causality: to wit, Every event has a cause.

It is admitted, that originally, this principle is not given in this form. What is given? Some particular event, and the judgment,— This particular event had a cause. It is also admitted and affirmed, that the universal principle is not, here, as is true of contingent general principles, given by the succession of particulars. For if you suppose the event repeated a thousand or a million times, all that you have in each instance is the particular event, and the particular affirmation,—This event had a cause. How then shall we account for the formation of the idea or principle under consideration? Let us recur to the individual fact above alluded to—the fact composed of two parts; the empirical and absolute parts. We will leave out of view the idea of succession, and confine ourselves to the one fact before us.

By immediate abstraction let us suppose the separation of the empirical, and the disengagement of the necessary and absolute. We then have the pure idea of the absolute and necessary. This idea, thus developed, we find it impossible not to apply to all cases, real or supposed. We have then, and in this manner, the universal, necessary, and absolute idea or principle.

This process might perhaps be more distinctly explained by a reference to the ideas of body and space. These ideas are not originally given in their present simple, abstract form. They are given in such propositions as this: This particular body is somewhere, or in space. Here you have the empirical part, body, and the necessary and absolute part, space. Separate the two, and you have the contingent idea of body, and the necessary and absolute idea of space. Hence the principle, universal, necessary, and absolute: Body implies space.

CLASSIFICATION.

The process of classification can now be readily explained. We will refer back to the case when two particular notions were in the mind, and the general was evolved from them. As soon as the notion last named appears, the two particulars are subsumed or classed under it. In the same manner every particular previously perceived is arranged under the general, and in all the successive modifications which it subsequently undergoes.

FORMS OF CLASSIFICATION.

There are three distinct points of view from which objects are classified.

1. In view of general resemblances, they are classed, on the ground of common qualities, under general notions, such as, man; animal, etc.

2. In view of some one quality without reference to resemblance in any other particular, they are classed under notions purely abstract, such as redness, whiteness, etc. We often class objects together, as white, hard, sweet, etc., without reference to their relations, in any other particulars.

3. Objects are classed together, in view of their correspondence to pure rational conceptions, such as, a circle, square, right and wrong, etc.

CLASSIFICATION, IN WHAT SENSE ARBITRARY.

It will readily be seen that classification from one point of view, will run directly across and break up that which is formed from another. How distinct and opposite, for example, will the classification be which is founded upon some one abstract quality, such as, redness, from that which is based upon general resemblance, and formed under a general conception. Equally distinct and unlike either of the others will be the arrangement of objects, which are classed together under some pure rational conception.

For these reasons classification has, by many been regarded as perfectly arbitrary. It is true, that we are at liberty to adopt either of the principles of classification above described we please. In this respect, the process is perfectly arbitrary. If we classify at all, however, we must adopt one or the other of the forms under consideration, no other forms being conceivable. When we have selected our principle, also, the subsequent arrangement of objects in conformity to it is necessary. In, very important respects, therefore, classification has its laws, which are by no means arbitrary.

GENERA AND SPECIES.

In the process of classification, objects are ranged together as genera and species. Thus we have the genus tree, and the different classes, or species of fruit-bearing and forest trees, ranged under it. A species also is often itself a genus relatively to particular and distinct classes belonging to that species. If fruit-bearing be assumed as the genus, then we have the apple, plum, peach, cherry trees, etc., ranged as species under this generic term. The illustration might be extended indefinitely, from the highest to the lowest forms of genus and species. Our present concern is with the *principle* on which objects are thus classed. It is that to which we have frequently referred in this chapter—the idea of *resemblance and difference.* The genus is formed on the perception of remote resemblances. Species under the genus are formed on the perception of important differences; while objects are classed under the species, on the perception of resemblances more near and special. Thus the genus tree is formed on the perception of qualities common to all trees. The species fruit-bearing and forest trees, are separated from each other, on the perception of important differences, each species being formed on the ground of resemblances more near and particular than those designated by the general term tree.

In illustration of the process in which classes, as genus and species, are formed, we will take the case of the child. A certain object stands near the paternal mansion, which he has learned to designate by the term tree. By and by he sees another object resembling this in all important particulars. Here, he says, is another tree. In his mind they are distinguished as greater and less, and in respect to location. Here is the obscure development of the ideas of genus and species. At length, however, he perceives a tree differing in very important particulars from either of the others. He

89

now asks the question, what *kind* of tree is this? The answer is, we will suppose, a maple tree. Then the inquiry arises, what tree is that which stands near the house? He is told that it is an elm tree. He has now the idea of the genus tree, formed on the perception of common qualities, and of two species, separated from each other on the perception of important differences. All trees subsequently perceived, presenting similar resemblances and differences, will be separated and arranged accordingly. As other trees, differing from either of these, are perceived, they will be separated and classed in a similar manner. Throughout the whole process, one idea guides the mind, that of resemblance and difference.

GENERALIZATION.

But few words are requisite in the explanation of the mental process called generalization. A general fact is a quality common to every individual of a given class. It may be peculiar to that class: or, while it belongs to each individual of the class, it may appertain to individuals of other classes.

RULES IN RESPECT TO GENERALIZATION.

1. No fact must be assumed in general, which does not belong to each individual of the class to which it is referred.

2. No general fact must be assumed as *peculiar* to one class, which, though strictly general in respect to that class, nevertheless appertains to individuals of other classes.

3. No fact must be assumed as general without a sufficient induction of particulars, to remove all doubt in respect to the question whether it is, or is not, a general fact.

INFERRED JUDGMENTS OR REASONING.

All judgments are characterized as intuitive, or inferred or deduced. The former we have already considered. To the latter class special attention is now invited. Two subjects, we will suppose, are in thought before the mind. The relations between them are not immediately, that is, intuitively discernible. How can these relations become objects of knowledge? On this one condition exclusively, that they sustain known and common relations of resemblance or difference, or unlikeness, equality or inequality, to some known object. So far forth as they, in the same particulars, agree with this one object, they do, and must, agree with each other. So far forth, on the other hand, as in the same particulars, one agrees and the other disagrees with this object, they disagree with each other. All valid deductions, all forms of valid reasoning, in all the sciences, have their exclusive basis in these principles. All the axioms, in all particular sciences, are nothing but these principles stated in forms adapted to said sciences. All reasoning which strictly conforms to these principles must be valid, and all such procedures which violate these principles must be invalid.

FORM OR BASIS OF ALL VALID DEDUCTION, OR REASONING.

From the nature of the case, as will be readily apprehended, every deduction, inference, or conclusion, in reasoning, must have its basis in two, and only two, propositions, called in science, premises: to suit, the general principle as above stated, and the facts of agreement or disagreement in conformity to said principle: —the inference or conclusion is thence deduced. The proposition containing the general principle, is called the major premise, that affirming the facts of the case, is called the minor premise; and that containing the inference, the conclusion. As in every argument there are two,—only two objects (terms) compared with a common third object (term), every valid argument must have two premises, and three terms. That with which these objects (terms) are compared is called the middle term, and those compared with said middle term, are denominated the extremes.

THE SYLLOGISM.

An argument expressed in regular form, is called a syllogism. If we assume the letters Z and X, to represent the extremes, and the letter M, to represent the middle term, an argument in syllogistic form would stand thus:

Every M is X.

Every Z is M.

Therefore, every Z is X.

91

While it is true, that very few arguments assume the form of the syllogism, it is also true, and self-evidently so, that all valid arguments are reducible to this form.

FIGURE OF THE SYLLOGISM.

The figure of the syllogism, as the words are employed in the science of logic, refers to the relations which the middle term sustains to the extremes in the premises of the syllogism. As in one of the premises one extreme is compared with the middle term, and with the other in the other premise, there are but three possible relations of subject and predicate which three such terms can sustain to each other. In the two premises, that term of which the other is affirmed or denied is called the subject, and that which is affirmed or denied of it is called the predicate. The relations referred to are these; to wit, that in which the middle term is the subject of one extreme and the predicate of the other,—that in which it is the predicate of both, and that in which it is the subject of both. As a consequence, there can be but three legitimate figures of the syllogism; the idea set forth in the common treatises on logic, that there is a fourth figure, being an important error in this science. We will give an example of a syllogism in each of the figures in order:

First figure.	Second Figure.	Third Figure.
$M = X.$	$X = M.$	$M = X.$
$Z = M.$	$Z = M.$	$M = Z.$
$Z = X.$	$Z = X.$	$Z = X.$

We have given the above syllogisms in these forms to demonstrate to the pupil a fundamental error in the common treatises on logic; to wit, that in the second figure, we can prove only negative, and in the third only particular, conclusions; whereas, in each figure alike, we legitimately obtain not only particular, but universal, affirmative conclusions. In the treatise on logic, as the reader will clearly see, by carefully studying Sir William Hamilton's scheme of notation given on page 162, we have absolutely demonstrated the fact, that in each figure in common, we obtain, in the most valid forms, twelve affirmative, and twenty-four negative, conclusions; and all in the same forms in each figure.

DISTRIBUTION OF TERMS.

A term is said to be distributed, when it represents, in the proposition in which it is employed, all its significates, that is, all the individuals of the class to which said term is applicable. In the proposition, all men are mortal, for example, the term men represents every individual of the race, and is, therefore, distributed. A term is undistributed, as is the case with the term men, in the proposition, some men are mortal, when it stands for but a part of its significate.

CONSTITUENT ELEMENTS OF PROPOSITIONS.

All logical propositions, being of course affirmative or negative, universal or particular, are composed of three parts,—the *subject,* that of which something is affirmed or denied,—the *predicate,* that which is affirmed or denied of the subject, and the *copula,* that by which the affirmation or denial is made. In the proposition, for example, X is M, X is the subject, M is the predicate, and *is* the copula,—the copula always being represented by the verb to be, in some of its forms.

RULES FOR THE DISTRIBUTION OF TERMS.

The following rules universally obtain in respect to the distribution of terms:

1. All universal and no particular propositions distribute the *subject;* thus constituting the fundamental distinctions between such propositions.

2. When the subject represents an inferior, and the predicate a superior conception, then *all negatives,* and *no affirmatives,* distribute the predicate. The reason for this rule is obvious. In the proposition, for example, all men are mortal beings, the term men represents one species, of which mortal beings are the genus, or superior conception. As the latter term has a wider application than

the former, or inferior conception, the proposition, *all* men are mortal beings, would imply no more than that *some* mortal beings are men. In all such propositions, consequently, the subject is, and the predicate is not, distributed. In negative propositions, on the other hand, all of the subject is denied of all the predicate, as in the proposition, no men are mortal beings. Here, of course, each term is distributed, because each represents all of its significates.

3. In all propositions, in which the subject and predicate are not related to each other as inferior and superior conceptions, all universal propositions distribute the predicate as well as the *subject.* In such propositions, for example, as these, X = M, A resembles B, and things equal to the same things are equal to one another, the terms or conceptions are equal and not inferior, the one to the other. As a necessary consequence, the predicate as well as the subject is distributed.

CONVERSION OF PROPOSITIONS.

A proposition is converted when its terms are transposed; that is, when the subject is put for the predicate, and the latter for the former. The proposition, before conversion, is called the *exposita,* and after conversion the *converse.* When there is a mere transposition of the terms, with no change of the quantity of the proposition, conversion is said to be *simple.* When there is a change of *quantity,* it is called conversion *by limitation.* In conversion, this rule holds, universally and for self-evident reasons, that no term must be distributed in the converse which was not distributed in the exposita. All forms of conversion in which this rule is not violated, are allowable. Hence the following specific rules of conversion have universal validity.

SPECIFIC RULES OF CONVERSION.

1. In all propositions in which neither term is distributed, as in all particular affirmatives; or in which both terms, the subject and predicate; are distributed, conversion may be simple. For example:

PARTICULAR AFFIRMATIVE.

Ex.—Some men are liars.

Con.—Some liars are men.

UNIVERSAL NEGATIONS.

Ex.—No patriot is a traitor.

Con.—No traitor is a patriot.

UNIVERSAL AFFIRMATIVES.

Ex.—Things equal to the same things are equal to one another.

Con.—Things equal to one another are equal to the same things.

2. In universal affirmative propositions in which the subject is an inferior, and the predicate the superior conception, conversion is by limitation; that is, the exposita is a universal, and the converse is a particular proposition. The converse of the proposition, all men are mortal beings, for example, is this: some mortal beings are men. This, from the nature of the case, does, and must, hold true in respect to all propositions of this character.

3. Particular negative propositions are converted by attaching the term of negation to the predicate. The converse of the proposition, some men are not honest, is this: some beings who are not honest are men. This is called conversion per accident. As in reasoning, there is very frequent occasion to use the converse of the proposition which has been proved, it is of great importance that the scientific student should fully comprehend the principles above elucidated.

FACTS AND PRINCIPLES IN SCIENCE.

The facts of science are those *events,* or *objects,* which admit of scientific explanation and elucidation. The principles of science are those self-evident truths, or *ascertained laws,* in the light of which the facts referred to are explained and elucidated.

RELATION OF FACTS TO PRINCIPLES OF SCIENCE.

Principles have validity for the explanation and elucidation of any given class of facts, when the validity of the former is necessarily *implied* by the latter; that is, when said facts are incompatible with any hypothesis but this, and all harmonize with it. The law of attraction, for example, as developed and elucidated by Newton, not only is consistent with all the facts of external nature, and explains them; but it is necessarily *implied* by them; all facts not only affirming its validity, but contradicting every other hypothesis. That law therefore, becomes legitimately a *principle* of science, for the scientific explanation and elucidation of the facts of nature. The same holds true of all valid principles of science. Their validity as such principles, is *necessarily implied* by the facts to the elucidation of which they are applied.

THE IMMEDIATE CONDITIONS OF VALID DEDUCTIONS IN SCIENCE.

All valid deductions in science are the necessary *consequents* of *valid* principles and *real* facts,—facts and principles sustaining to each other the relations above designated. Deductions not having their exclusive basis in such principles and facts, have no claim to validity.

HYPOTHESES AND ASSUMPTIONS IN SCIENCE.

An hypothesis, as distinguished from a principle in science, is a supposition or idea *assumed* to account for known facts; but not necessarily implied as true by said facts. An hypothesis, to be worthy of any regard whatever, must be consistent with all the facts to which it is applied, and rationally explain them all. An hypothesis may be properly employed in the explanation of facts when it is definitely understood that it is employed only as an hypothesis, and when said facts do not reveal and verify principles for their own consideration. An hypothesis, also, shown to be consistent with a given class of facts, has absolute validity against any deductions based upon an opposite hypothesis pertaining to the same facts. A class of facts is adduced, for example, to prove the crime of murder. The facts adduced to prove the charge, and the arguments based upon said facts, are proved to be utterly void of validity, when it is shown, that these facts are all consistent with some opposite hypothesis,—mere accidents, for example, or the motive of self-defense. Facts equally consistent with various and opposite hypotheses, prove neither, in distinction from any of the others. *Assumptions* are *mere hypotheses,* employed as *valid principles* in the explanation of facts, and the construction of systems of knowledge. All unascertained facts, employed as real and known, in the construction of such systems of knowledge, having their basis in assumptions, are mere logical fictions. Such, —as we have demonstrated in the science of Natural Theology especially,—are the fundamental characteristics of all the, various systems of materialism, idealism, skepticism, naturalism, and evo- lution. When we examine the basis principles of every one of these systems, we find those principles to be, without exception, mere assumptions,—utterly void of all claims to the high rank of *principles of science.* And yet this is the exclusive form in which they are employed in the construction of those systems.

THE JUDGMENT, HOW IMPROVED.

The judgment is developed and improved, by means of a habit of careful discrimination in respect to objects of thought,—noticing their points of resemblance and difference: by the habit of careful classification and generalization, and of the equally careful refer- ence of facts to principles. One of the most eminent mathema- ticians that this country ever produced, laid the foundation of his high attainments, by careful study of a single work,—the common arithmetic. Finding himself, on his entrance into college, uniformly deficient and behind his class, especially in the mathematics, he went back and took up the treatise referred to, and studied it until he had not only solved every problem presented, but fully com- prehended every principle and rule in the science as therein treated; and furthermore, the reasons and grounds of the *validity* of the rules and principles. The result was, that from that the onward no member of his class, and no student in the institution, could keep in sight of him in any department of the mathematics. Such are the immutable conditions of attaining a strong and well balanced judgment; and no individual who thus thinks and studies can fail to attain this high power. Not a few students become immutably disciplined in the science of non-thinking, by the careless and indiscriminating and incomprehensive study of "many books."

FUNDAMENTAL ERROR IN PHILOSOPHY.

In most treatises on Mental Science, no proper distinction is made between these two faculties, the understanding and judgment. Coleridge, for example, defines the understanding as "the faculty of judging according to sense." Reason he also defines and elucidates as the faculty of apprehensions and judgment in respect to necessary truths. Hence, he affirms that "judgments of the understanding admit of degrees, while those of reason preclude all degrees." Other philosophers who have treated at all of these faculties, have adopted the same conclusion. Hence, they often speak of "the *logical understanding";* while reason is represented as the proper *scientific* faculty,—the faculty employed in all the pure sciences. Now neither the understanding nor the reason are, in any sense, faculties of judgment. By the understanding, we form *conceptions,* or *notions* of the objects of external and internal perceptions. By the reason, we apprehend the realities necessarily *implied* by objects of perception,—realities, such, for example, as space, time, substance, and cause. By the faculty of judgment, we affirm the *relations* existing between the objects thus perceived and apprehended. By the understanding, for example, we form conceptions of body. By reason, on occasion of forming such conceptions, we apprehend space. By the judgment exclusively, we affirm the *relations* existing between these two objects, body and space; a relation expressed in the proposition, body implies space. The same holds true in all other instances. We have but one scientific faculty,—the judgment; and this faculty is exclusively employed in all judgments and deductions; in all the sciences alike, pure and mixed; and in affirming relations between all objects and realities, finite and infinite. "Confusion worse confounded" is introduced into the sphere of science, when these distinctions are overlooked, or misapprehended.

CHAPTER VIII.

ASSOCIATION.

TERM DEFINED.

"That one thought is often suggested to the mind by another, and that the sight of one external object often recalls former occurrences, and revives former feelings, are facts," says Mr. Dugald Stewart, "which are perfectly familiar, even to those who are least disposed to speculate concerning the principles of our nature." This is what is meant by the term *association.* It is that principle of our minds by which past thoughts and states are recalled, and revived, through the influence of present perceptions, thoughts, and feelings. This law of the human mind was denominated by the old philosophers, "association of ideas." By Dr. Brown it was denominated "suggestion." By others, it is designated by the simple term, association.

TERM ASSOCIATION, WHY PREFERRED.

I prefer the latter term to either of the former, because it alone expresses all the phenomena which require consideration, when treating of the subject before us. We find by experience, that not only thoughts and events are associated, but thoughts, events, and feelings also. The term association of ideas, can be properly applied to ideas only. The same is true of suggestion. An idea or event cannot properly be said to suggest feelings. Thoughts and events may be said to revive feelings; and feelings may be said to suggest thoughts and events. Association is the term, and the only term, which can properly be applied to all these different classes of phenomena.

THE ASSOCIATING PRINCIPLE NOT WITHOUT LAW.

Although the mind is so constituted, that certain states follow certain other states, these phenomena, as philosophers have long since observed, not only do not follow each other at random, but are known to follow some one or more fixed laws. To ascertain and illustrate the operation of these laws, has been considered one of the great problems in intellectual philosophy; and has, accordingly, occupied a conspicuous place in almost every treatise upon the science. Mr. Hume, I believe, was the first philosopher who attempted to settle definitely the number of these laws. According to this philosopher, they are all reduced to three: Resemblance, cause and effect, and contiguity in time and place. Others have since added that of contrast.

THE LAW OF ASSOCIATION.

Years ago, Dr. Brown presented the suggestion,—a suggestion which he did not attempt to verify, that "if our analysis be sufficiently minute" all associations would be found to depend upon one and the same law. Mr. Dugald Stewart had previously affirmed, that there are great numbers of facts of association that do not fall under any of the laws developed by any of his pre-decessors. "Things," he says, "which have no known relations to each other, are often associated, in consequence of their producing *similar effects* upon the mind." Here Mr. Stewart, without being aware of the fact, has stated the only, the exclusive, and universal, law of association.

THE LAW OF ASSOCIATION STATED.

Whenever any one object of present thought, or perception, suggests something else which has been a former object of thought, or perception, the reason, and the only reason is, that the present object produced upon the mind an effect similar to that which was produced by the former object.

That this is the only and exclusive law I argue from two fundamental considerations.

PHENOMENA OF ASSOCIATION EXPLAINED.

1. All the phenomena referred to the commonly received laws, can be explained on this hypothesis.

That many of the phenomena of association can be accounted for in consistency with the commonly admitted laws, will be denied by no person of reflection. That objects which resemble each other, that those which have been perceived at the same time or place, that sustain to each other the relation of *contrast,* or cause and effect, do mutually suggest each other,—is undeniable. But do such phenomena necessarily suppose the existence of a plurality of laws? May they not all be referred to one, and that the one under consideration? Those of resemblance, obviously may. The same is true of those which sustain to each other the relations of contiguity of time and place, and of cause and effect. For they undeniably have co-existed with the same feeling or states of mind. The only phenomena which present the appearance of difficulty, are those of *contrast.* That a giant and a dwarf resemble each other in but few particulars, and that they stand in striking contrast to each other, is readily admitted; but that, as objects of perception, or recollection, they may have co-existed with the same feelings, or states of mind, and as causes also of the same, I as fully believe, as I do that the conception of a hero and of a lion have co-existed in a similar manner. A giant and a dwarf are strongly contrasted; but each, as striking departures, though in different directions, from the common stature, may have co-existed with similar feelings of *wonder* or *surprise,* and as common causes of the same; and this may be the only reason why one suggests the other. In conversing upon this subject on a particular occasion, an individual present remarked, that he recollected having, at a particular time, seen a dwarf. A giant, which he had previously seen, was not suggested at all, but another dwarf whom he had before met with. I at once asked the speaker, if the giant referred to was not a familiar acquaintance of his. He replied that he was. This fact readily accounted for the phenomena of association, presented by him. Familiarity had destroyed the feeling of strangeness, which had formerly co-existed with the perception or recollection of the giant. The same feeling, however, co-existing with the perception of the two dwarfs, the perception of one would of course suggest the other. In the same manner, all the phenomena of contrast may be reduced to the hypothesis before us.

FACTS OTHERWISE INEXPLICABLE.

2. There are fundamental facts of association which can not be accounted for, except by the law under consideration.

This is admitted by Mr. Stewart in the extract above cited, and his statement will be denied by no one at all familiar with facts of consciousness. I will now adduce some facts of this kind.

1. *Facts of analogy,*—an exceedingly various class of associations, which can be accounted for best upon this one principle. Why, for example, do the conception of the lion and of the hero, mutually suggest each other? Externally they bear no relations of resemblance, contiguity in time or place, cause and effect, or contrast. The contemplation of one, however, does produce upon the mind awe inspiring effects similar to those which are induced by the contemplation of the other, and this is the only assignable reason why they mutually suggest each other. So of all other facts of association. An individual, for example, relates to a number of persons a single incident of a sublime, beautiful, heroic, horrid, or ludicrous character. How happens it that each hearer instantly recollects almost every incident of a similar character which he has ever met with? These incidents resemble each other in one particular only, and sustain no other relation to each other than this: they have, as objects of perception or contemplation, existed in the mind as causes of similar feelings to those awakened by the incident under consideration. The hypothesis before us is the only one conceivable which accounts for such phenomena.

2. *Phenomena of Dreaming,*—The phenomena of dreaming can readily be accounted for on this hypothesis, and, as I conceive, upon no other. In consequence of peculiar attitudes of the body, or states of the physical or mental system, certain feelings are awakened in the mind. Those objects of thought or perception which have formerly co-existed with similar feelings, are consequently suggested; and these are judged to be the causes of existing feelings. A sick man, for example, with a bottle of hot water at his feet, dreamed that he was walking upon the crater of Etna, and that this was the cause of the burning sensation which he felt. He had formerly felt similar sensations when walking upon the crater of Vesuvius, and had just been reading of a traveler's walking -upon

the crater of Aetna. These facts fully account for his dream. In a similar manner, all the phenomena of dreaming may be accounted for. But can they be accounted for by the common laws of association? I answer, no.

3. *Phenomena of Somnambulism,*—Some of the phenomena of somnambulism here deserve an attentive consideration. It is well known that somnambulists frequently pass from a state of wakefulness to that of sleep, and *vice versa,* very suddenly; and that in each change, there is an entire oblivion of what passed in the preceding state; while the train of thought, or the employment left, when passing from the present state, is, on returning to that state, instantly resumed, at the very point where it was left. Sentences left half finished, when passing out of one state, are completed as soon as the individual enters upon the same state again. How manifest, from such phenomena, is the fact, that the universal law of suggestion is based upon similarity of states or feelings.

FACTS CONNECTED WITH PARTICULAR DISEASES.

There are many facts connected with particular diseases, which more fully confirm and illustrate the principle which I am endeavoring to establish. Take, as a specimen, the two following cases stated by Dr. Abercrombie, in his Intellectual Philosophy. I give them in the words of the author.

"Another very remarkable modification of this affection is referred to by Mr. Combe, as described by Major Elliott, professor of mathematics in the United States Military Academy at West Point. The patient was a young lady of cultivated mind, and the affection began with an attack of somnolency, which was protracted several hours beyond the usual time. When she came out of it, she was found to have lost every kind of acquired knowledge. She immediately began to apply herself to the first elements of education, and was making considerable progress, when, after several months, she was seized with a second fit of somnolency. She was now at once restored to all the knowledge which she possessed before the first attack, but without the least recollection of anything that had taken place during the interval. After another interval she had a third attack of somnolency, which left her in the

103

same state as after the first. In this manner she suffered these alternate conditions for a period of four years, with the very remarkable circumstance that during the one state she retained all her original knowledge; but during the other, that only which she had acquired since the first attack. During the healthy interval, for example, she was remarkable for the beauty of her penmanship, but during the paroxysm wrote a poor, awkward hand. Persons introduced to her during the paroxysm, she recognized only in a subsequent paroxysm, but not in the interval; and persons whom she had seen for the first time during the healthy interval, she did not recognize during the attack."

"Dr. Prichard mentions a lady who was liable to sudden attacks of delirium, which, after continuing for various periods, went off suddenly, leaving her at once perfectly rational. The attack was often so sudden that it commenced while she was engaged in interesting conversation, and on such occasions it happened, that on her recovery from the state of delirium she instantly recurred to the conversation she had been engaged in at the time of the attack, though she had never referred to it during the continuance of the affection. To such a degree was this carried, that she would even complete an unfinished sentence. During the subsequent paroxysm, again, she would pursue the train of ideas which had occupied her mind in the former. Mr. Combe also mentions a porter, who in a state of intoxication left a parcel at a wrong house, and when sober could not recollect what he had done with it. But the next time he got drunk, he recollected where he left it, and went and recovered it."

Here are manifest and striking facts of association. On the commonly received laws of the associating principle, they cannot be explained at all. On the hypothesis under consideration, however, they admit of a most ready explanation. How can they be explained on any other hypothesis?

I will adduce another fact taken from the same author.

"A case has been related to me of a boy, who at the age of four received a fracture of the skull, for which he underwent the operation of trepan. He was at the time in a state of perfect stupor, and after his recovery retained no recollection either of the accident or of the operation. At the age of fifteen, during the delirium of a fever, he gave his mother a correct description of the operation, and the persons who were present at it, with their dress, and other minute particulars. He had never been observed to allude to it before, and no means were known by which he could have acquired the circumstances which he mentioned.

But one explanation can be given of such a remarkable fact. During the interval between the surgical operation and the sickness referred to, the feelings existing in connection with the operation had never been revived, and from the peculiarity of the feelings could not have been. During this sickness, in consequence of the action of the fever upon the brain and skull, these feelings were revived. The consequence was, that the circumstances attending their existence were recalled. No other hypothesis can explain such facts.

WHY DIFFERENT OBJECTS EXCITE SIMILAR FEELINGS.

The law of associations has been stated and illustrated. We are now prepared for another important inquiry, to wit, On what principle is it that *different objects,* or rather thoughts and perceptions, excite *similar feelings* in our minds, and thus mutually suggest each other? The following may be specified as the most important reasons why different objects excite such feelings.

1. In consequence of natural *resemblance* between the *objects themselves.* That objects naturally alike should excite similar feelings, is a necessary consequence of personal identity. Such objects do not suggest one another, because they are alike, but simply because, being alike, they excite similar feelings. The principle of association in such instances is the same as in all others.

2. Objects excite similar feelings, and thus mutually suggest each other, in consequence of *similarity of relations to the original principles of our nature.* Sweetness, beauty, and harmony, as mere objects of sense, are totally unlike. But they may and do sustain such a relation to the original principles of our nature, as to induce similar states of mind. Consequently, the perception of one may suggest that of the other. Thus the origin of figurative language,

such as sweet or beautiful sounds, admits of a ready explanation. Also the sublime comparisons of poetry and oratory; founded upon the relations of analogy. An Indian orator, speaking of the American revolution, said, "That it was like the whirlwind, which tears up the trees, and tosses to and fro the leaves, till we cannot tell whence they come, nor whither they will fall. At length the Great Spirit spoke to the whirlwind, and it was still." Says another, whose age numbered more than one hundred years: "I am the aged hemlock. The winds of an hundred winters have whistled through my branches, and I am dead at the top." "And I heard," says the sacred writer, "as it were the voice of a great multitude and as the voice of many waters, and as the voice of mighty thunderings, saying, Alleluiah; for the Lord God omnipotent reigneth." Milton, speaking of the breaking up of the council of Pandemonium, says:

> "Their rising all at once, was as the sound
> Of thunder heard remote."

An aged soldier, in one of the tragedies, says of himself:

> "For I have fought when few alive remained,
> And none unscathed; when but few remained.
> Thus marred and mangled—as belike you've seen
> O' summer's night, around the evening lamp,
> Some scorched moths, wingless, and half consumed
> Just feebly crawling o'er their heaps of dead."

How different, as mere objects of sense, are all the things compared together in the above quotations! But sustaining a common relation to the original laws of the mind, they induce similar feelings or states of mind. Consequently, the apprehension of one, suggests that of the other.

3. Objects co-exist and excite similar feelings, in consequence of a perceived relation between the objects themselves; such, for example, as the relations of cause and effect, parent and child, etc. Why it is that the feelings excited by one of these objects are transferred to the other as soon as the relation between them is perceived, we cannot tell. All that we can say is, that such is the constitution of our minds, that when two objects are known to sustain such relations to each other, they will, in all ordinary

106

circumstances, excite similar feelings and the idea of one will, consequently, suggest that of the other.

4. Objects co-exist with similar feelings in consequence of mere accidental association. Whenever the mind has been brought, from any cause whatever, into any particular state, the accidental perception of any object, or suggestion of any thought, however foreign to the cause of the present state, will so modify that state, that the new object will ever after sustain an entirely new relation to the sensibility of our nature. To the present state of the mind, thus modified, it sustains the relation of a cause. Consequently, its subsequent presence as an object of perception, or of conception, will excite, in a greater or less degree, that state, and will of course recall the objects which formerly co-existed with the same state. Thus the same object may, at different periods of our lives, be associated with entirely different, and even opposite states of mind, states of mind, also, totally different from what they are naturally adapted to produce. Thus of course they may and will, recall entirely different objects to our remembrance. In many instances, we find it wholly impossible to account for the change which has taken place in the effect of particular objects upon our sensibility, and consequently upon our train of associations; so gradual and accidental, has been the transfer of the object from one state of feeling to another.

APPLICATION OF THE PRINCIPLES ABOVE ILLUSTRATED.

The law of association which has been confirmed and illustrated, has many and very important *applications.* To a few of these, special attention is invited, as we conclude the present chapter.

GROUND OF THE MISTAKE IN RESPECT TO THE LAWS OF ASSOCIATION.

We are now prepared to state distinctly the ground of the mistake of philosophers, pertaining to the laws of association. Because objects sustaining certain relations to each other do mutually suggest one another, they have fastened upon these relations as the *laws* of association. In this manner, they have overlooked the fact, that objects suggest each other, only on the ground of a common impression made by each upon the mind, and that the relations existing between them present the reason why they make a common impression, instead of revealing laws of the associating principle. Philosophers have noticed the fact, that some objects are associated on the exclusive ground of a common impression. Yet they have singularly overlooked the universal law of association revealed in that fact.

ACTION OF THE ASSOCIATING PRINCIPLE IN DIFFERENT INDIVIDUALS.

We are all familiar with the fact, that the action of the associating principle is very different in different individuals. This is evidently owing to two circumstances,—natural temperament, and the diverse pursuits of individuals; one thereby being more deeply interested in, and consequently more deeply impressed with different objects, and with different elements of the same object, than another. Let any number of individuals of diverse temperaments, for example, contemplate the same painting, each will be most forcibly impressed with those features of it particularly correlated to his own peculiarities of natural temperament. Hence the corresponding diversity of the action of the associating principle, in such a ease. So with a gentleman on a tour of observation; a merchant engaged in the purchase and sale of grain; and a farmer seeking a location for his family;—in looking over the same plantation. Each will contemplate it in the light of the leading idea in his own mind. A corresponding diversity will of course exist in the impressions received, and in the consequent action of the associating principle.

INFLUENCE OF HABIT.

That actions and trains of thought, to which we have been long familiar, are performed and carried on by us with a degree of ease and exactness perfectly unaccountable to a new beginner, is obvious to every one. In respect to the ease and exactness with which trains of physical actions to which we have become habituated are repeated, two reasons may be assigned.

The first is, a certain conformation of the physical organization so that, as soon as the train is commenced the action of the muscles in obedience to the will is spontaneous and necessary in a given order of action.

The second is, the fact that all the actions under consideration have become indissolubly associated with the same state of mind. Of course, as soon as that state is reproduced, those actions are spontaneously suggested in their proper order.

The same remarks are equally applicable to trains of thought to which we have become habituated. When the mind has often existed in a certain state, there is, as shown above, a strong tendency, spontaneously, or on the slightest impression to recur to that state again. The train of thought having become associated with this state is, of course, pursued with precision and facility.

STANDARDS OF TASTE AND FASHION.

"A mode of dress," says Dugald Stewart, "which at first appears awkward, acquires, in a few weeks or months, the appearance of elegance. By being accustomed to see it worn by others whom we consider as models of taste, it becomes associated with the agreeable impressions which we receive from the ease and grace and refinement of their manners," Thus the pronunciation common to the higher classes in Edinburg, while it remained the capital of Scotland, and which was then regarded as the standard of purity in diction, has now become barbarous, in consequence of the removal of the capital to London.

VICISSITUDES IN RESPECT TO SUCH STANDARDS.

Every one is familiar with the perpetual vicissitudes in dress, and everything, the chief recommendation of which is fashion. The remarks of Mr. Stewart on this point also, are so much to the purpose, and so well expressed, that I will venture another citation from him. "It is evident that, as far as the agreeable effect of ornament arises from association, the effect will continue only while it is confined to the higher orders. When it is adopted by the multitude, it not only ceases to be associated with ideas of taste and refinement, but it is associated with ideas of affectation, absurd imitation, and vulgarity. It is accordingly laid aside by the higher orders, who studiously avoid every circumstance in external appearance, which is debased by low and common use; and they are led to exercise their invention in the introduction of some new peculiarities, which first become fashionable, then common, and last of all are abandoned as vulgar." There is one circumstance which Mr. Stewart has not mentioned, which has perhaps quite as much influence in inducing these vicissitudes as that presented above. "The higher classes" are pleased with revolutions in society which are visibly produced by themselves, and which do not diminish, but increase and render manifest, to themselves and the world, their own controlling influence. In the perpetual vicissitudes of costume, proceeding from and controlled by themselves, they are continually manifested to themselves as the "glass of fashion, and the mould of form." Thus a continued gratification of the love of power is enjoyed, a motive not the most commendable to be sure, but yet quite as real as that above presented.

PECULIARITIES OF GENIUS ASSOCIATED WITH JUDGMENT, OR CORRECT TASTE.

We are now able to state distinctly the peculiarities of true genius, when associated with good judgment. It consists in distinguishing those things which please,—simply in consequence of accidental associations, like those above referred to,—from those which are correlated to the original and changeless principles of our nature; and in thus shadowing forth the real and permanent forms of beauty, sublimity, and fitness. Those forms of thought which stand correlated to the current opinions of the day, may have a wide-spread ephemeral popularity, after which they sink to a silent or dishonored grave, and a long oblivion. The productions of true genius, associated with good taste; on the other hand, will please as long as human nature remains what it is.

INFLUENCE OF WRITERS AND SPEAKERS OF SPLENDID GENIUS, BUT OF INCORRECT TASTE.

It is well known, that very strong conceptive and imaginative faculties (the peculiarities of true genius), sometimes exist in the absence of a well balanced judgment and consequent good taste. The productions of such individuals will be characterized by surpassing excellences, and glaring defects. Yet the mass of their admirers will, in time, become as well pleased with the latter as with the former; and the defects will, perhaps, be more frequently copied by imitators than the excellences. The reason is this. The defects come to be associated with the feelings of interest and delight which the excellences excite. The former are thus embalmed and consecrated by the latter. Every individual who would preserve his taste unvitiated, should be, in a special sense, on his guard under such circumstances.

DANGER OF VICIOUS ASSOCIATIONS.

Great genius and great vices, polished manners and corrupt morals, and productions the most finished in respect to style and imagery, and the most foul in respect to sentiment, are not unfrequently associated among men. The imminent peril of intercommunion with such minds and with such productions, is manifest, in the light of the law of association above illustrated. The feelings of sublimity, beauty, and delight, awakened by the contemplation of great minds, polished manners, and the perfections of style and imagery,—at first weaken, and finally entirely supplant the feelings of disgust, abhorrence, and repellency, which the contemplation of vice and corrupt principle, in their unassociated grossness, excites. The final result is, the acquirement of polished manners and style, with the loss of virtue and virtuous principles. That "which cannot be gotten for gold," and for "which silver cannot be weighed as the price thereof," in comparison with which "no mention shall be made of coral or of pearls, and the price of which is above rubies," has been exchanged for that which might have been attained in much higher perfection without this irreparable loss; but which may exist in connection with the foulest morals, and an equal preeminence in guilt.

UNFOUNDED PREJUDICES, HOW JUSTIFIED.

Every individual is familiar with the fact, that person and classes of men, placed in circumstances degrading in public estimation, often become the victims of cruel and unrighteous prejudice. Some circumstance, aside from condition, is fastened upon as the cause of this feeling, which is thus justified, on the assumption that it is natural, and therefore necessary, designed and sanctioned by Providence. Feelings connected with individuals by accidental association, are assumed as resulting from the original constitution of our nature, and are justified on that assumption.

SLANDER AND LIBEL.

It is very frequently asserted as a proverb, that the evils resulting from giving persons a bad name, and spreading false reports respecting them, will ere long correct, and more than correct themselves, in consequence of a reaction of public feeling, as the truth comes to be known. This would be true, were men disposed to render impartial justice in all instances. But this is far from being the case. Preeminent virtues and endowments, together with a commanding influence, may often, under such circumstances, occasion a reaction of public feeling which will perfectly overwhelm the authors of the mischief. The standing of the mass of mankind, however, is not such as to occasion such reaction, even when the wrong done comes to be known. Hence, it often happens that the feelings first awakened come to be permanently, to a greater or less degree, associated with them in the public mind. If this is not so, no thanks are due to those who first set the ball rolling.

INFLUENCE OF ASSOCIATION IN PERPETUATING EXISTING MENTAL CHARACTERISTICS.

"To the pure," says the sacred writer, "all things are pure; but to the corrupt and unbelieving, there is nothing pure." In other words, a mind truly pure comes to be so correlated to objects in respect to not only the action of the voluntary power; but also in respect to the sensibility and intelligence, that all things awaken thoughts and feelings tending to perpetuate and increase that purity. The same is true with the vicious. Every object of thought and perception is brought into such a relation to their minds, as to generate thoughts and feelings which tend only to develop and confirm existing tendencies to corruption. This law of self-perpetuation which virtue and vice respectively possess, is found in the associating principle. In a mind which has long been the cage of impure thoughts and feelings, those feelings at last come to be associated with all objects of thought, and thus the entire current of thought and feeling is turned into an impure channel.

There are no limits to the application of the associating principle, as above illustrated. Its importance in mental science will be appreciated as it is understood in its endlessly diversified applications.

CHAPTER IX.

MEMORY AND RECOLLECTION.

Memory and Recollection are treated by philosophers, as important departments only of the principle of association. This, as we shall see, is demanded by sound philosophical analysis. The two terms above named are often used interchangeably, and never distinguished but by the following circumstances. In the process denominated *memory,* notions, or conceptions of facts and events, are spontaneously recalled to the mind. In that called *recollection,* these intellectual states are recalled by an effort of will.

STATES OF MIND IN MEMORY AND RECOLLECTION.

There are three distinct mental operations connected with each of these processes of mind.

1. Some feeling or state of mind which has formerly co-existed with the perception or apprehension of the object recalled—a feeling or state spontaneously recurring, or revived by some object of present thought, perception, or sensation.

2. A simple apprehension of the object or event itself,—an apprehension attended with no belief or judgment whatever pertaining to the object.

3. A recurrence, in thought, of the circumstances of time and place connected with the perception or apprehension of the object.

THE ABOVE STATEMENT VERIFIED.

That objects of memory and recollection are not recalled directly and immediately, but are suggested, in the manner above described, is obvious from two considerations.

1. From universal *consciousness.* Those who are least accustomed to analyze the operations of their own minds, as well as philosophers, have noticed the fact. Hence the common affirma-

tions: "this reminds me of," or "this suggests to my mind such and such occurrences,"—clearly showing, not merely that such events are suggested, but that the objects of them are conscious of it.

2. When we wish to recollect any events, or in the common phrase, to recall them; we do not attempt to do this directly, but by directing the attention to various objects, at present before the mind, that they may suggest those which we wish to recall. Memory and recollection are, in this respect, subject to precisely the same law; and the law which governs each is the same which governs the entire phenomena of association. The above remark is so obviously true, that philosophers, as stated above, almost universally treat of these subjects in the same connection, memory being considered as one department only of association.

DISTINCT AND EASY RECOLLECTION.

Taking this position for granted, or as having been already proved, it will follow, as a necessary consequence, that the *ease* and *distinctness* with which any objects or events will be recalled to the mind, will always be proportioned, to the depth and intensity of the impressions formerly received from them, and to the number of objects and events with which such impressions have heretofore co-existed, or may hereafter co-exist. This conclusion we also find to be confirmed by universal experience. When you hear the declaration, "such and such events I shall never forget," suppose you ask the reason for such an affirmation. The answer will invariably be, "it made such a deep impression upon my mind." On the other hand, if a person is asked for the reason why he recalls with such difficulty any particular event, he will uniformly answer, "it made such a feeble impression upon my mind." Assuming that the state of the sensibility is the regulating principle of suggestion, the fact is self-evident, that the ease with which any particular event will be recalled, depends not only upon the depth and intensity of the impression which it formerly made, but upon the number of objects or events with which such impression may have coexisted, and will hereafter co-exist.

DISTINCT IMPRESSIONS, ON WHAT CONDITIONED.

One inquiry, of no small importance in mental science, here claims our attention, to wit, the circumstances under which impressions received from objects of thought or perception are rendered deep and distinct. Among these I notice the three following, as the most important:

1. At*tention.* In former chapters it has been shown that attention is the condition of distinct perception, in respect to the phenomena of both sense and consciousness. In walking, for example, we do not remember the particular act of volition, which directed each particular step. Yet we know that we must have been conscious of such acts. The eye runs carelessly over a particular landscape, and nothing but the most general outline is remembered, while we know that each particular part must have been seen by us. For the want of attention, however, these objects were not distinctly perceived. Of course no distinct and vivid impression was made upon the mind, and consequently they are not remembered. The manner in which attention influences memory is two-fold. It not only impresses deeply and distinctly on the mind particular scenes, each taken as a whole, but all the parts of such scenes. Hence the whole of such scenes will be recalled by the perception or suggestion of any particular part, which may be met with in other scenes. That memory, however, does not depend primarily upon attention, but upon the *impression* made by objects of attention, is evident from the fact, that the ease with which any particular event is recalled, is not proportioned to the degree of attention devoted to it, but to the vividness of the impression received from it.

2. The impression made upon the mind by a particular event and consequently the ease with which it will be recalled, depends upon the *circumstances* in which the event occurred—circumstances external to the mind; such for example, as its occurrence at a time and place unexpected; in connection with other events deeply interesting to us, etc.

3. The impression which events make on the mind, depends upon the state of the mind itself, when they occur. Offices of kindness, when we little need them, make a comparatively slight impression upon the mind. They are accordingly forgotten with

comparative ease. But the stranger who watched over us when we were sick, in a strange land, we never forget; for the obvious reason that such occurrences are deeply impressed upon the mind. Who is not aware that the impression made upon the mind in reading a book, listening to a discourse, or witnessing any scene, and consequently the ease and distinctness with which they are recalled, depends greatly upon the state of mind at the time?

DIVERSITY OF POWERS OF MEMORY, AS DEVELOPED IN DIFFERENT INDIVIDUALS.

Assuming the principle, that those things of which we have formed distinct conceptions, and which have deeply moved and affected our sensibility, will be easily and distinctly remembered, the diverse kinds of memory, as they appear in different individuals, may be readily explained.

PHILOSOPHIC MEMORY.

The philosopher is, above all things, interested in universal truths and general principles, and in facts which illustrate such truths and principles. With names, and minor circumstances of time and place, he has little or no interest. These, of course, he seldom recalls; while general principles and facts connected with, and illustrative of general principles, he never forgets. Here we have the peculiarities of what may be called *philosophical memory.*

LOCAL MEMORY.

With general principles, however, the mass of men are very little interested. Events, as mere events, with all their circumstances of time, place, etc., are the things which chiefly interest them. In such cases, general principles, if understood at all, will readily pass from the mind, while facts and events, with all their adventitious circumstances, will leave their permanent impress upon it. Here we have the characteristics of what is called *local memory.*

ARTIFICIAL MEMORY.

The third and only other kind of memory which it is necessary to notice, is called *artificial memory,* a method of connecting things easily remembered with those which are recalled with greater difficulty, that the latter may be recalled by means of the former. The manner in which the principle of suggestion operates in this instance, may be readily explained. The two objects are brought into the relation of co-existence with one and the same state of mind; and the familiar object, by exciting that state, recalls the one less familiar. The inexpediency of resorting to such associations, excepting upon trivial subjects, is so obvious as not to need any particular remarks.

A few topics of a somewhat miscellaneous character, connected with our present inquiries will close this chapter.

A READY AND RETENTIVE MEMORY.

The distinction between what is called a ready, and a retentive memory, next demands attention. A philosophical memory is known to be the most retentive and least ready. General principles are regarded by the philosopher, as above all price. These of course he never forgets. For the same reason, facts and events, connected with, and, illustrative of general principles leave an impress equally permanent upon his mind. The memory of such a person however, will not, in ordinary circumstances, be ready; for the obvious reason, that when he wishes to recall any particular fact, he finds it necessary first to recall the general principle with which it was associated. For the same reason, *local* memory will be more ready, but less retentive. The qualities in objects with which such persons are interested, exist alike in such an infinite variety of objects, that when this quality is met with, a great multitude of similar objects will be at once suggested. They will generally be those however, which have been most recently seen. Persons possessing local memory merely, will excel in common conversation, and in what may be called loose and rambling composition. Philosophical memory, displays itself in the laboratory, the hall of science, on the bench, in the lecture room, and pulpit.

118

The degree in which this faculty is developed in different individuals, may now be readily accounted for. It is owing, as I suppose, to two circumstances—natural diversities in which the power is possessed by different individuals, and the accidental direction of the power. Themistocles knew every citizen of Athens by name. Cyrus and Hannibal had each a similar knowledge of every soldier in his respective army. Their original endowments made them capable of such acquisitions. They made such acquisitions, because they considered them necessary to the end they designed to accomplish.

IMPROVEMENT OF MEMORY.

But for the faculty under consideration, the past would be to us, as if it had not been. No advantages could be derived from experience of our own or that of others. Existence, at each successive moment, must be commenced anew. The same errors and follies, which formerly occurred, must be repeated, without the possibility of improvement. Through this faculty, the past furnishes the chart and compass for the future. The progress of improvement is onward, with perpetually accumulating force. The question, therefore, How can this faculty be improved? presents itself, as of special importance. The following suggestions may not be out of place on this point:

1. The first thing to be kept distinctly in mind, in all plans for the permanent improvement of memory, is the principle on which its ready and retentive action depends; to wit, deep and distinct impression. All our plans for the accomplishment of the object under consideration, should be formed with direct reference to this one principle.

2. As impressions depend very much upon distinctness of conception, in all efforts to improve this faculty, we should habituate ourselves to form distinct conceptions of objects, especially of those which we wish to recollect. In this manner the impression will not only be deep and permanent, but the notion associated with

it being distinct, will, when recalled, possess a corresponding distinctness.

3. In thought, the object should be located in distinct relation to the circumstances of time and place with which it is associated. In this manner the impression and conception will not only be rendered deep and distinct, but each circumstance referred to, as it recurs in connection with other thoughts and perceptions will, by exciting the feelings under consideration, recall the object associated with it.

4. Knowledge, in order to be retained permanently, must be systematized and reduced to general permanent principles. Otherwise, it will be exclusively subject to the law of local association which is so temporary in respect to retention.

5. To converse with others, and to write down our thoughts which we wish to retain, contribute to permanency and distinctness of recollection. Knowledge, by this means, is rendered distinct, the corresponding impression deep and permanent, and the whole subject of thought, most likely to be systematically arranged. All these circumstances tend to render memory distinct and permanent.

6. Memory also, to be improved, must be trusted, but at the same time, not overburdened, as is the case when everything is communicated to it, without the aid of a judicious diary of important thoughts and occurrences. That faculty which is not exercised will not be developed and improved. Memory is not exempt from this law. At the same time, to overburden a faculty is a sure way to palsy its energies. Nothing but reflection and judgment, properly exercised, can fix upon the line where memory should and should not be trusted, without the aid of written records of our thoughts, and thus secure a proper development of this faculty.

MEMORY OF THE AGED.

One of the first indications of the approaching feebleness of age, is the failure, in a greater or less degree, of the power of memory. A characteristic precisely the opposite is also sometimes presented in the experience of aged persons,—a wonderful revival of the memory of the occurrences of early life. A lady of my acquaintance, for example, aged about ninety years, had occasion to amuse some of her great-grandchildren one day. She thought she would, as a means to this end, relate to them the substance of a story, related in verse, which she had read when quite young. She had never committed it to memory, and doubtless had thought little of it for more than half a century. As she commenced the story, the entire poem came fresh to her recollection. She could repeat it all, word for word. These two facts in the experience of the aged,—the failure of memory, on the one hand, and its wonderful revival, on the other, need to be accounted for.

In respect to phenomena of the first class, two reasons may be assigned for their existence:

1. The failure of the faculty of *perception* and *attention.* As a consequence, distinct notions are not formed of objects of present thought and perception. Nor do they affect the mind as they formerly did. For these reasons, the peculiar feelings which have co-existed with former thoughts and perceptions, and would, if revived, suggest them, are not revived.

2. In the failing of the perceptive faculty, there is a corresponding change in the correlation of the *sensibility* to objects of thought and perception. Hence not the same feelings precisely are now excited by objects of thought and perception, as formerly, and consequently former intellectual states are not reproduced.

In respect to the second class, I would remark, that every one is aware, that amid the hurrying scenes of ordinary life, such crowds of associations rush upon the mind, at one and the same time, that no one entire scene of the past, is often distinctly recalled. On the other hand, when we are in a state of temporary isolation from the varying tide of events which is floating by and around us, then, is the time when our recollections of the past become full and distinct. Now the aged are in a state of isolation of a more permanent character. Hence, when a past scene is recalled, the mind is in a state of comparative freedom from all diverting and distracting associations. Consequently, the scene, in its entireness, is brought into full and distinct remembrance.

DURATION OF MEMORY.

If the law of association illustrated in the preceding chapter be admitted as true, it will follow, as a matter of course, that memory is absolutely indestructible. Thought can never perish. If the impression with which any thought has co-existed, should, at any period, however remote, be in any form revived, the thought itself may be recalled. If any element of a given impression be reproduced, no reason can be assigned, why a thought which co-existed with it, myriads of ages ago, should not thereby be recalled, as well as the one which co-existed with it but yesterday.

Numberless facts also, which lie around us in society, fully confirm the principle under consideration as a law of memory. The case of the aged lady referred to above, presents a fact of this kind. The most striking one that now recurs to my recollection is given by Coleridge. It is the case of a German girl who had always labored as a domestic. While Coleridge was on a visit to Germany, and in the vicinity of her residence, she sickened, and if I mistake not, died. During her sickness, she began to utter sentences in languages unknown to all her attendants. Learned men, from a neighboring university, were called in. It was then found that she was reciting, with perfect correctness, entire passages from the Hebrew, Greek, Arabic and Syriac scriptures, and also from the writings of the ancient Fathers. The occurrence was, by many, regarded as miraculous. A young physician in attendance, however, determined to trace out her past history, for the purpose of finding a clue to the mystery. He found at last, that when quite small, the young woman had lived in the family of an aged clergyman of great learning, who was in the daily habit of reading aloud in his study from the writings above referred to. As the child was at work in a room contiguous, she was accustomed to stop, from time to time, and listen to those strange sounds, the meaning of not one of which did she understand. There was the clue to the mystery. Those sounds were imperishably impressed upon the memory. Hence their repetition, under the circumstances named. Cases of a similar nature might be adduced to any extent. They point with solemn interest to the nature of the immortal powers within, as well as to facts of portentous moment in the future development of those powers.

CHAPTER X.

THE IMAGINATION.

All are aware, that there is such a function of the intelligence as that designated by the term *imagination*. When, also, we meet with any of its real creations, we readily recognize them as such. But, when the questions are asked,—What is this power? What are its proper functions? and, By what *laws* is it governed? the true answer,—that which will command general assent, does not so readily occur, as, at first thought, might be anticipated. If we recur to the works of authors who have attempted to define and elucidate the subject, we find that they differ so 'widely in their definitions of this faculty that little satisfactory information is obtained from their presentations.

By some, we are told, that the real function of the imagination, is to "present the objects of pure perceptions in groups and combinations which do not exist in nature," or to "take the component parts of real scenes, events, or characters, and combine them anew, by a process of the mind itself, so as to form compounds which have no existence in nature."

By others, it is defined as the faculty by which we "modify our conceptions, by combining the parts of different ones together, so as to form new wholes of our own creation"; or as "a complex exercise of the mind, by means of which various conceptions are combined together, so as to form new wholes." The difficulty which the student meets with in respect to such definitions, is the impracticability of determining, in their light, whether, when he meets with a given conception, he is in the presence of a real creation of the imagination or not. Without further remarks we shall now attempt a definition of our own.

IMAGINATION DEFINED.

An object of which our apprehensions are indistinct, may often be best defined and explained by comparing it with some other analogous object of which our apprehensions are distinct and well defined. The imagination, as all admit, is a conceptive faculty. So is the understanding, and of this latter faculty we are well informed. Let us compare these two faculties, and see if we cannot, thereby, obtain clear and distinct apprehensions of the real and proper functions of each. The understanding, as we have seen, combines the elements given by the primary faculties, sense, consciousness, and reason, *as* given, without modifying them at all; its exclusive province being this: to conceive of, and represent in thought, objects as they are in themselves, whatever their nature and characteristics may be. A conception of the understanding we always compare with its object, and pronounce said conception perfect or imperfect; as it does, or does not, perfectly represent that object. Now we have another and different faculty of conception, a faculty which re-combines the elements of thought given by all the other faculties; and blends said elements into conceptions which correspond, more or less perfectly, not with realities as they are in themselves, but with certain fundamental ideas in the mind,—ideas such as those of harmony, fitness, the beautiful, the grand, the sublime, the good, and the perfect; or their opposites, the ludicrous, the grotesque, and the bombastic. We have in our minds, therefore, two entirely distinct classes of conceptions,—those which respect objects just as they exist in the universe of matter and mind, within and around us; and those in which the elements of such objects are in thought combined, in harmony, more or less perfect, with fundamental ideas in the mind itself; as those of the beautiful, grand, sublime, etc.,—conceptions which do not respect objects as they are, but certain arrangements of such objects. The function of the intelligence which gives us the former class of conceptions, we have denominated the understanding. That which gives us the latter is the imagination. By Coleridge it is called the "Esemplastic, or into-one-forming power." It re-combines the elements of thought into conceptions which pertain, not to mere existences; but to ideas of the beautiful, the perfect, the sublime, etc., in the mind itself. A conception of the understanding is perfect, when it represents its object as it is, whatever the object may be. A conception of the imagination is perfect, when it shadows forth forms of beauty, grandeur, sublimity, etc, which correspond with the ideas in the mind. Understanding conceptions are compared with the *object*. The only standard with which the creations of the imagination are compared, is the *idea*.

ILLUSTRATION.

A single illustration will throw additional light upon the distinct and separate functions of these two faculties under consideration. A number of human forms and circumstances, each characterized by greater or less beauties and deformities, are, we will suppose, before the mind. Of each, and of all together, we form distinct apprehensions; the group, with all its individualities, being, in thought, represented as it is in itself. Here we mark the exclusive action of the understanding. While these objects are before the mind there arises, in thought, the apprehension of a human form and countenance more beautiful and perfect, than any which had been the object of perception or conception before. The formation of this new conception is the equally exclusive creation of the imagination. The same holds true in all other instances. Wherever, and whenever, we find the elements of thought, given by the other faculties, re-combined into conceptions which correspond, not with realities as they are in themselves, but with fundamental ideas, pre-existing in the mind itself,—ideas such as the beautiful, the grand, the sublime, etc., we here find ourselves in the exclusive presence of creations of the imagination. Such creations, as we shall see hereafter, may, or may not, be fictions, may, or may not, be true to objects which have existence in nature. Such creations, however, whether true to real existences or not, will always present their objects in the light of the ideas referred to.

IMAGINATION AND FANCY DISTINGUISHED.

Mr. Dugald Stewart is the first philosopher that I have met with, who makes a distinction between the imagination and the fancy. I will give the remarks to which I refer, as it will prepare the way for the distinction which I wish to make. "It is the power of fancy," he observes, "which supplies the poet with metaphorical language, and with all the analogies which are the foundation of his allusions.

But it is the power of the imagination, that creates the complex scenes he describes, and the fictitious characters which he delineates." According to the distinction here made, it was the imagination of Milton, which created the whole scene, and the particular characters, presented in "Paradise Lost." His fancy, on the other hand, furnished the figurative language, analogies, and illustrations, with which it is adorned. The fancy, as thus described, is, as it will readily be perceived, nothing but a particular department of the operation of the principle of association. It collects the materials from which the imagination creates its scenes and characters, and then furnishes the attendant embellishments. In conformity to this view of the subject, fancy is defined by Coleridge, as the "aggregative and associative power." Thus defined, while the imagination is that function of the intelligence which is correlated to ideas of the beautiful, the grand, the sublime, etc.,— the fancy is that function of the associative principle, which is correlated to the same ideas.

SPONTANEOUS AND REFLECTIVE IMAGINATION.

The *primitive* action of the intellectual faculties, is spontaneous, and not reflective. We reflect upon that only which has a prior existence in the mind. The same statement is applicable to all the creations of the imagination. In their primitive developments, they are the result of the spontaneous action of this faculty. By reflection, such creations are, subsequently, fully developed and perfected. The grand conception, for example, developed in "Paradise Lost," was first spontaneously suggested to the author's mind. To fill out and perfect that conception, was the object of thought and study for a majority of the years of his subsequent life.

REMARK OF COLERIDGE.

Coleridge has somewhere made a remark, which I regard as of great importance in guiding the judgment in detecting the peculiar operations of the imagination, and in separating them from the operations of other intellectual faculties. The amount of his remark is this. It is not every part of what is called a production of the imagination, that is to be attributed to that faculty. Much, often, is mere narration; and much is the mere filling out of the grand outline of the conception which the imagination has combined; and which as properly belongs to the understanding and judgment, as the filling up of the outlines of any other discourse of which the intelligence has conceived. With a great portion of the filling up of "Paradise Lost," for example, imagination had no more to do than with that of filling up the grand outline of a sermon, or oration. In the sublime conception itself, and in the mysterious blending of the elements of thought often met with, in throwing that conception into form,—here we find the workings of this creative, plastic faculty. To evolve principles which would enable the student, under such circumstances, to discern the operations of this faculty, has, as before said, been the main object of the preceding analysis.

CREATIONS OF THE IMAGINATION, WHY NOT ALWAYS FICTIONS.

In the preceding part of this chapter, it has been shown, that the creations of the imagination are not always, as it has often been stated by philosophers, "new wholes which do not exist in nature." It becomes an important inquiry, When and why is not this statement true? It will be evident, at first thought, that when the elements of thought which enter into particular conceptions, are wholly recombined, the new wholes, thus produced, must exist purely in thought, without any corresponding existence. On the other hand, when the elements of beauty, grandeur, and sublimity exist in objects in connection with other and different elements,— elements related to other and different ideas, and when the imagination blends these elements first named into some one beautiful, grand, or sublime conception, every element in the conception may be in strict correlation to realities. Take as an illustration, a single stanza from a familiar hymn:

> "His word of grace is sure and strong,
> As that which built the skies:
> The voice that rolls the stars along
> Speaks all the promises."

Every element in this beautiful thought is strictly conformed to realities, as they are. Yet in the blending of these elements, particularly in the last two lines, we distinctly mark the plastic power of the imagination, in its sublimest and most beautiful form.

The same is equally true, where the same power embalms, in similar conceptions, the hallowed sentiments and experiences of the past, and present. Who that ever saw the tear of gratitude lying in the eye of affliction,—a thing far more beautiful than the dew-drop, when it holds in its embrace the image of the morning sun,—a tear started by some gift that eased, for a time, the pressure of woe, and, then turned away with a sorrowful heart, that such worth should be crushed beneath such a weight, does not recognize the truth, as well as beauty, of the thought contained in the following stanza, especially in the last two lines?

> "I have heard of hearts unkind, kind deeds
>   With coldness still returning:
> Alas! the gratitude of men
> Has oftener left *me* mourning."

In another sense, all the proper creations of the imagination are true. They are true to thought. In the depths of our inner being, there lie thoughts too deep for any words which we can command. Nothing but an overshadowing imagination can call them forth, and give them an external embodiment. Whether the forms in which they are embodied are correlated to substantial realities or not, they are true to thought, the most important of all realities. We feel grateful, therefore, when we find the thoughts which we had vainly endeavored to express, molded into form, and thus assuming "a local habitation and a name."

I mention one other, and a very important sense, in which the creations of the imagination are true. They sustain, in many instances, relations to realities analogous, somewhat, to that sustained by general notions. In a very important sense, these last have no realities in nature corresponding to them; that is, there is no one object, that in all respects corresponds to a general notion; that is, that contains the elements it represents, and nothing more nor less. The elements belonging to it, however, are found in each particular object ranged under it. Let us now, in the light of this illustration, contemplate the forms of the beautiful, for example, shadowed forth by the imagination. We may not be able, in all instances, to find any one particular object which contains, and nothing more nor less, the elements which enter into this form. Yet, whenever we meet with an object containing the elements of beauty, we find that element represented in the forms of the beautiful bodied forth by the imagination. In these forms, we do not find any one particular shadowed forth, but each particular blended in the universal. In the most perfect forms of statuary, for example, we do not find any one human form, in distinction from all others, represented, but we find whatever is beautiful in every form there embodied. As the understanding represents the particular in the general, so the imagination represents all particulars relating to the beautiful, etc., in the universal.

SPHERE OF THE IMAGINATION NOT CONFINED TO POETRY.

Most of the examples introduced into this chapter are poetical. From this I would not have it supposed, that, in my judgment, the imagination is confined to this species of composition. We meet with its finest creations, on the other hand, in painting, in statuary, in prose, and in every kind of discourse in which the elements of thought can be blended in harmony with pure ideas. It admits, at least, of a doubt, whether the imagination of Milton ranged with a more discursive energy in his highest prose compositions, or in his "Paradise Lost."

LAW OF TASTE IN REGARD TO THE IMAGINATION.

It is, as we have seen, the peculiar province of the imagination to dissolve, re-combine, and blend the elements of thought. Its procedure in all these respects, however, is not arbitrary. Not every thought can be blended with every other, without violating the laws of good taste. Here, then, an important question presents itself; to wit, What is the law which guides the imagination, in blending the elements of thought? I will present my own ideas on this subject, by an example taken from the book of Job:

"Hast thou given the horse his strength?

Hast thou *clothed his neck with thunder?*"

129

The propriety of blending the two conceptions,—that of the mane of the war-horse and of thunder, has been questioned by some, on account of the total dissimilarity of the objects of those conceptions. It is readily admitted, that no two objects are in themselves more dissimilar. Yet it is confidently maintained, that there never was a figure of speech more appropriate. The reason is obvious, and everyone feels it, though he may not have an analytical consciousness of it. When two objects are, as objects of sense, totally dissimilar, the conception of each may excite precisely similar feelings. Hence the propriety and force of the figure employed by the sacred writer, in blending the two conceptions into one. This I conceive to be the universal law of good taste, relative to the action of the plastic power of the imagination. Whenever two conceptions sustain a similar relation to any one common feeling or sentiment, they may be blended into one. The more diverse the objects of those conceptions, the more striking the figure, under such circumstances. I will give one other example:

> "The twilight hours like birds flew by,
>   As lightly and as free
> Ten thousand stars were in the sky,
>   Ten thousand in the sea;
> For every wave with dimpled cheek
>   That leaped upon the air,
> Had caught a star in its embrace,
>   And held it trembling there."

Who is insensible to the exquisite beauty of the thought here? Yet the wave of the sea or lake, reflecting the stars of night, no more, as an object of sense, resembles the dimpled cheek of beauty, or the mother catching up her babe and holding it in her embrace, than the mane of the war-horse resembles thunder. Why, then, are we struck with such delight at the blending of conceptions, the objects of which are, in themselves, so unlike? The answer is, these conceptions are mutually correlated to the same or similar feelings. When such conceptions are thus blended into a beautiful emotion common to both, there is shadowed forth the perfection of beauty. For this reason our hearts leap up, when we meet with such thoughts as the following, taken from the same effusion as that above cited:

"I have heard the laughing wind behind,
When playing with my hair—
The breezy fingers of the wind,
How cool and moist they were!"

IMAGINATION THE SOURCE OF IDEALS.

Another important function of the imagination now claims our attention, its function as the source of ideals. In illustrating this function, the first thing to be accomplished is to distinguish between ideals and ideas.

IDEA DEFINED.

An idea, properly defined, is a conception of reason. As such it has the characteristics of universality and necessity, and is consequently, incapable of change, or modification. Thus whenever certain conditions are fulfilled, reason evolves the idea of time, space, substance and cause, which we have already considered, together with such as the beautiful, the right, the true, and the good, etc., hereafter to be considered.

IDEAL DEFINED.

An ideal is a form of thought intermediate between an idea and the conceptions or notions which the intelligence generates of particular objects, and presents archetypes in conformity to which the elements of such conceptions may be blended in harmony with ideas. In the mind of Milton, for example, the ideas of the beautiful, the grand, and the sublime, etc., existed as pure conceptions of reason. When the varied conceptions, the elements of which are blended together in "Paradise Lost," lay under the eye of his consciousness, his intelligence, brooding over those elements, at last blended them together into that grand conception, of which the poem itself is the external embodiment. This conception was the ideal after which the poem was formed, to realize his ideas of the grand, the beautiful, and the sublime.

IDEALS, PARTICULAR AND GENERAL.

Ideals, like notions, are particular and general. Thus, in the mind of Milton, there existed a general ideal of what a poem should be, in order to realize, in greater or less perfection, the pure ideas of reason. At the same time, there existed a particular ideal of the manner in which the elements entering into that poem should be blended, in order, in that particular production, to realize those ideas.

IDEALS NOT CONFINED TO IDEAS OF THE BEAUTIFUL, THE GRAND, AND THE SUBLIME.

Ideals are not confined to any one class of ideas. Every individual, in all departments of human action, has an ideal of the form to which the objects of his action should be brought into conformity, and in the light of which he judges of all productions which meet his eye. Ideas of fitness, of the true, the perfect, and the good, no less than the idea of the beautiful, are the archetypes of ideals.

IDEALS NOT FIXED AND CHANGELESS LIKE IDEAS.

Ideals, as compared with ideas, may be perfect or imperfect. They are consequently capable of continued modifications. We often hear it said of individuals, that their ideals are imperfect or wrong. As intermediate archetypes between conceptions of particular objects, and pure ideas of reason, ideals may, in the progress of the intelligence, undergo endless modifications, always advancing towards the perfect and absolute, without reaching it.

IDEALS THE FOUNDATION OF MENTAL PROGRESS.

As intermediate archetypes between particular conceptions and universal and necessary ideas, ideals constitute the foundation of endless progression in the development of the mental powers. Every new elevation which the intelligence gains, presents new conceptions of particular objects, and consequently new elements of thought. Every new element of thought involves a new ideal, more nearly approaching the perfect and the absolute, and thus lays the foundation for fresh activity, and further progress in the march of mind. Sometimes also ideals degenerate, and thus the foundation is laid for the backward movements of society.

It is hardly necessary to add that the imagination is the sole originator of ideals. To form such conceptions is not a function of reason, nor of the understanding or judgment. It remains, then, as the exclusive function of the imagination.

IDEALS IN THE DIVINE AND HUMAN INTELLIGENCE.

In the divine mind, the action of the imagination is always in perfect and absolute correspondence to the reason. As a consequence, there is a similar correspondence between the divine ideal and idea. All of God's "works, therefore, are perfect." Not so with the finite. Man may eternally progress towards the infinite and perfect, but can never reach it.

TASTE DEFINED.

Taste is that function of the *judgment* by which the characteristics of productions, especially in belles-lettres and the fine arts, are determined in the light of *ideals and ideas* of beauty, order, congruity, proportion, symmetry, fitness, and whatever constitutes excellence in such productions. The judgment may be exercised upon ideals relatively to ideas, and upon particular productions relatively to both. Thus Milton, when he apprehended the conception realized in " Paradise Lost," might, and doubtless did, often compare that conception with his own idea, to determine the fact whether the former made a near approach to the latter. In filling out the conception, he would continually compare the external embodiment with the internal ideal. In all such operations, he was exercising those functions of the faculty of judgment denominated *taste.* The existence of good taste depends upon the existence in the intelligence of correct ideals, together with a well balanced, and well exercised judgment, pertaining to the ideas of beauty, fitness, etc. If a man's ideal is false, his taste is of course vitiated. If his ideal were ever so correct, and he was not possessed of a well balanced, and well exercised judgment, pertaining to such productions, he would also lack the characteristics of good; taste.

By Asa Mahan.

PRODUCTIONS OF THE IMAGINATION WHEN NOT REGULATED BY CORRECT JUDGMENT OR GOOD TASTE.

In some individuals, in whom the imagination exists and operates with a high degree of energy, its action is not guided and chastened by good taste, or a well regulated judgment. In such cases we find the most perfect forms of beauty and sublimity shadowed forth in connection with the grossest deformities. The subject also will, in most instances, be wholly unable to distinguish the one from the other. In listening to such men, we, at one moment, are perfectly electrified with the forms of beauty, grandeur, and sublimity which are shadowed forth to our ecstatic vision; but the next, perhaps, we are equally shocked and disgusted with images worse than grotesque, and forms of speech in strange violation of all the laws of good taste. Under such circumstances we have special need of two things, patience and good judgment. The former will enable us to endure the evil for the sake of the good; the latter to separate the one from the other; that we may not, as is too often the case, receive the good and the bad, as alike good, nor reject both as alike bad.

The most perfect of all human productions are the results of genius associated with good judgment. Of these the productions of Milton may be referred to as striking examples. Grandeur and sublimity are the permanent characteristics of his genius. And how seldom are his sublime conceptions marred with violations of good taste!

PRODUCTIONS OF IMAGINATION AND FANCY.

The productions of different authors, we read with almost equal interest, but for entirely different and opposite reasons. I now refer to two classes of productions only, in one of which the operation of the fancy is most prominent, and in the other, that of the imagination. In productions of the former class, there will be an exuberance of metaphor, and beautifully appropriate comparisons and illustrations, and these will be the main source of the interest felt. In contemplating the productions of a creative imagination, on the other hand, the grand, *conception* will be the chief, and in some instances, the exclusive source of interest.

IMAGINATION AND FANCY—HOW IMPROVED.

Every power is developed in one way only,—in being exercised upon its appropriate objects. Each of the functions of the intelligence under consideration, has its appropriate sphere. To develop the power, we must find its legitimate sphere, and in that sphere exercise it upon its appropriate objects. The fancy is improved, by developing in the mind the sense of the beautiful, the true, the perfect, and the sublime; by furnishing the intelligence with distinct apprehensions of the forms of beauty, grandeur and sublimity which the universe of matter and mind, nature and art, presents.

The imagination will be improved by familiarizing the mind with the true functions of the power itself; with the laws which regulate its actions, in blending into form the elements of thought; and with its actual creations, as given in the works of minds most highly gifted with this function of the intelligence.

CHAPTER XI.

REASON RESUMED.

In former chapters it has been shown, that reason sustains this relation to the faculties of sense and consciousness: It gives the logical antecedents of phenomena affirmed by these faculties. Thus, on the perception of phenomena, we have the ideas of time, space, substance, personal identity, and cause.

Now reason sustains a relation to the understanding precisely similar to that which it sustains to sense and consciousness. It gives the logical antecedents of notions and conceptions, as well as of primary intuitions. The idea of right and wrong, of obligation, is not the logical antecedent of mere phenomena given by sense and consciousness. Before obligation can be conceived of or affirmed, the notion or conception, not of mere phenomena but of an agent possessed of certain powers, and sustaining certain relations to other agents, must be developed in the intelligence. The idea of obligation, then, is not the logical antecedent of phenomena affirmed by sense and consciousness but of notions given by the understanding. These considerations fully establish the propriety of the distinction between ideas of reason as primary and secondary. The former are the logical antecedents of phenomena given by the primary contingent faculties. The latter sustain the same relation to those of the secondary faculties. The distinction here made seems hitherto, as far as my knowledge extends, to have escaped the notice of the analyzers of the human intelligence. Its reality and importance to a correct understanding of the operations of the human mind will appear manifest as we proceed with our analysis of the secondary ideas of reason. An exposition of all the ideas comprehended under this class will not be attempted. All that will be attempted will be the induction and elucidation of a sufficient number of particulars to serve as lights to the philosophic inquirer, in his researches in the domain of mental science.

IDEA OF RIGHT AND WRONG.

Of the secondary ideas of reason, that which claims the first, and more special attention, is the one mentioned above, that of right and wrong, together with those dependent upon it, or necessarily connected with it.

UNIVERSALITY OF THE IDEA OF RIGHT AND WRONG.

It is an undeniable fact, that in the presence of certain actions, the human mind characterizes them as good or bad, right or wrong; that the mind affirms to itself, that one class of the actions ought, and the other ought not to be performed; that when we have performed certain actions, we deserve reward, and that when we have performed others, we deserve punishment; and that when this takes place, there is moral order, and when it does not, there is moral disorder. Such judgments are passed alike by all mankind, the old and the young, the learned and the ignorant, the savage and the civilized. Should it be said, that mankind differ in different circumstances in their judgment of the moral qualities of actions; I reply:

1. This objection itself implies the universality of moral distinctions. As men may differ in referring particular effects to particular causes, while all agree in the judgment that every event must have a cause, so it is with moral distinctions. Men may not always attribute the same moral qualities to the same actions; yet they universally agree in this, that our actions are either right or wrong.

2. But when we refer to intentions, in which alone the moral quality of actions consists, we find a more extensive agreement among men than is generally supposed. A man wills the good of an individual possessed of moral excellence. Where is the intelligent being in existence who does or can regard such an act as any other than virtuous? Who is not aware, that men, always justify wrong actions, if at all, by a reference to their intentions, showing by such reference, that in their judgment of the great law of love, all agree?

3. Vicious actions are seldom regarded as virtuous. Men may persuade themselves that it is not wrong to perform such actions, but never that they are bound to do them, or deserve a reward for having done them.

When an intention morally right is submitted to the contemplation of mankind, all agree in admitting it as virtuous and meritorious. Thus the sacred writer speaks of himself and associates, as through a "manifestation of the truth, commending themselves to every man's conscience." This could not have been the case, had not the consciences of all men been in fixed correlation to the moral law. The idea of right and wrong, then, is universal.

IDEA OF RIGHT AND WRONG NECESSARY.

It is also necessary. When the intelligence affirms an action or intention to be right or wrong, it is impossible to conceive of it, as possessed of the opposite character. We can no more form such a conception, than we can conceive of the annihilation of space. It has the same claim to the characteristics of universality and necessity, that any other idea has.

IDEAS DEPENDENT ON THAT OF RIGHT AND WRONG.

A moment's reflection will convince us, that the idea of right and wrong is the foundation of that of obligation; and this again, of that of merit or demerit; and this last of that of reward and punishment. When man would justify the bestowment of reward, or the infliction of punishment, they always refer to the merit or demerit of the individual. This judgment is sustained by a reference to the obligation of the same individual, and his obligations are shown by a reference to the idea of right and wrong. Such facts clearly indicate the relation of these ideas, the one to the other.

CHRONOLOGICAL ANTECEDENT TO THE IDEA OF RIGHT AND WRONG, ETC.

It has already been remarked, that the ideas under consideration are the logical antecedents, not of the phenomena of the primary contingent faculties, but of understanding conceptions. Before we can conceive of ourselves as subjects of moral obligation, we must be conscious of the possession of certain powers, and of existence in certain relations to other beings. This knowledge is the chronological antecedent of the ideas of right and wrong, while these ideas sustain to the facts of consciousness the relation of logical antecedents. The question now is, What are the elements of moral agency, necessarily presupposed as the condition of the existence of the idea of right and wrong of obligation, etc., in our minds? They are the following.

1. Power to know ourselves together with our relations.

2. The actual perception of such relations.

3. Power to act, or to refuse to act, in harmony with these relations.

That the ideas of right and wrong sustain to such conceptions the relation of logical antecedent, is evident from the following considerations:

1. When we conceive of a being possessed of these powers, and existing in such relations, we necessarily affirm obligations of him. An intelligent being is revealed to me, as possessed of capacity for virtue or vice, together with susceptibilities for happiness or misery. I have a consciousness of the power to will his virtue and happiness, or his vice and misery. I instantly affirm myself under obligation to will the former instead of the latter. No other conceptions are necessary to the existence of this affirmation. These facts also being postulated, obligation must be affirmed. We can no more conceive it right to will the evil instead of the good, or, that we are not under obligation to will the latter, than we can conceive of the annihilation of space.

2. If any of these elements are not postulated, obligation can not be conceived of, nor affirmed. If we deny of a creature intelligence to perceive his relations to other beings, we cannot conceive of him as under obligation to them. Whatever degree of intelligence be attributed to him, this involves, in our apprehensions, no obligation to one act of will instead of another, in the absence of all power to put forth the required, instead of the prohibited act. Suppose a creature has any degree of intelligence whatever. This creates no obligation to locomotion, in the absence of corresponding power. Suppose the mind located in a body totally destitute of the power of locomotion. Would the existence of intelligence create obligation to locomotion? Certainly not. Such would be the response of universal mind. Now the power to will is just as distinct from the

intelligence, as that of locomotion is. Hence, intelligence, of whatever kind or degree, can no more create obligation to one than the other, in the absence of corresponding power. To the conception of an agent, then, possessed of intelligence to know his relations, and power to act, or refuse to act, in harmony with those relations, the ideas of right and wrong, of obligation, etc., sustain the relation of logical antecedents.

IDEA OF FITNESS.

Every person who has attentively noticed the operations of his own mind, must have observed, that under certain circumstances, certain actions, or certain states of mind, appeared to him fit and proper. When asked to give a reason for such judgments, no other account can be given, than a simple reference to the nature of the thing itself; and to the circumstances supposed. For illustration, take the following passage of Scripture: "It was meet that we should make merry and be glad; for this thy brother was dead, and is alive again; and was lost, and is found." Suppose that father to have been required to give a reason for the judgment that under the circumstances supposed, joy and merriment were fit or proper. What answer could he have given? No other answer than for the judgment, that no phenomena exist without a cause. In both instances the mind knows absolutely that its judgments are, and must be true. No other reason for their truth, however, can be given, than this: The circumstances being given, they are self-affirmed.

THIS IDEA SYNONYMOUS WITH RIGHT AND WRONG, ETC.

Now the idea of fitness, when applied to moral relations, is identical with that of right and wrong. It is the foundation of the idea of merit and demerit; and consequently of that of reward and punishment.

It is also identical with the idea of moral order. When it is asked, why is that state in which virtue is rewarded and vice punished, regarded as a state of moral order? no other reason can be assigned than this: Such a state is fit and proper.

IDEA OF THE USEFUL, OR THE GOOD.

Whenever we conceive of a creature capable of pleasure or pain, happiness or misery, we necessarily conceive of a state in which all the capacities of such a creature for pleasure and happiness are perfectly filled. This state we designate by the term good, a term sometimes used in another sense, as synonymous with that of right. Whatever tends to fill out the measure of pleasure and happiness, we designate by the general term, useful.

The ideas of the useful and the good, above defined, give birth to all the varied forms of human industry, such as agriculture, the mechanic arts, commerce, etc. All are moving on to the realization of one great leading idea, the filling up of the capacities of man for pleasure and happiness.

THE SUMMUM BONUM.

There is one idea of reason, expressed by the words, the great good, the summum bonum, and the το χαλον, about which philosophers have long disputed, and in respect to which, they have been about equally divided in opinion. The question may be thus put: When we think of ourselves, or of the universe at large, what is that state to which our nature is correlated, as preferable to any other, actual or conceivable?

Some have placed the great good in happiness merely. To this position, however, we find that our nature is not exclusively correlated. If happiness were the only thing to which our nature is correlated, as in itself most to be desired, if happiness exists, we should be totally indifferent in respect to the means, or conditions of its existence. We are not pleased, but pained at the thought, for example, that perfect happiness should be associated with great wickedness.

Others, in departing from this idea, have placed the great good, in virtue. To this position, also, we find that our nature is not correlated. If virtue is the only thing that the mind regards as good, it would be indifferent in respect to the condition in which it should exist; whether, for example, the virtuous agent were happy or miserable. We are pained, on the other hand, at the thought, that

141

virtuous beings should not be happy. Happiness our intelligence affirms to be the right of the pure and virtuous.

The true solution is, no doubt, to be found in the blending of the two above given, or, as Cousin expresses it, "In the connection and harmony of virtue and happiness as merited by it." If we conceive of a state of perfect virtue, associated with perfect happiness, this conception contains a realization of our idea of the summum bonum. Every department of our nature is correlated to that idea. We can conceive of no state so much to be desired as this. Nor can we perceive any element in this state to which the laws of our being do not fully respond.

IDEAS OF LIBERTY AND NECESSITY.

These ideas, like those of right and wrong, are opposites. The elements entering into one, are excluded from the other. The question is, What are the characteristics which separate and distinguish one of these ideas from the other? In answer, I would remark, that they represent two entirely distinct and opposite relations, which may be supposed to exist between an antecedent and its consequent. The first is this: The antecedent being given, but one consequent is possible, and that must arise. This relation we designate by the term necessity. The second relation is, the antecedent being given, either of two or more consequents are possible, and consequently, when any one does arise, either of the others might arise in its stead.

IDEA OF LIBERTY REALIZED ONLY IN THE ACTION OF THE WILL.

The relation between all antecedents and consequents, with the exception of motives and acts of will, are conceived by the intelligence as necessary. If the idea of liberty is not realized in the action of the will, it exists in the intelligence without an object, or any element in any object corresponding to it, in the universe.

CHRONOLOGICAL ANTECEDENTS OF THESE IDEAS.

No idea of reason does or can exist in the mind, without the appearance of some phenomena, through which it is revealed. The existence of the idea of liberty can be accounted for only on the supposition of the appearance in consciousness of the element of liberty in the action of the will. In all other phenomena of which the mind is conscious, the element of necessity appears. The appearance of these phenomena, then, are the chronological antecedents of the ideas of liberty and necessity.

IDEA OF THE BEAUTIFUL AND SUBLIME.

All men agree in pronouncing some objects beautiful, and some sublime, and others the opposite. By many philosophers, the beautiful and sublime are contemplated as simple emotions. Some suppose, that all objects are to the mind originally alike in this respect, that they are unadapted to awaken any such emotions in the mind, and that these feelings come to be connected with particular objects by accidental association. Pleasing emotions are from some cause awakened in the mind. While in this state, we perceive, we will suppose, a rose. These emotions are thus associated with that object, so that when it is perceived again, they reappear. Hence, not because the rose is in itself more beautiful than any other object, but on account of the feelings thus associated with it, it is ever after regarded as beautiful. Now to this theory there exists this insuperable objection. Accidental association can never account for the absolute universality of judgment which exists among mankind, in respect to particular objects. Why, for example, do all the world agree in pronouncing the rose and lily more beautiful than the poppy or sunflower? Accidents never produce perfect uniformity.

Others suppose, that there are in the mind ideas of reason represented by the terms beautiful and sublime, and that objects are referred to one or the other, as they present corresponding characteristics. I will now present certain considerations designed to show, that this last is the true conception.

CONSIDERATION INDICATING THE EXISTENCE IN THE MIND OF IDEAS OF REASON, DESIGNATED BY THE TERMS BEAUTIFUL AND SUBLIME.

One fact which has a very important bearing upon this question, strikes the mind at first view. It is this: No human form or countenance is regarded by any person as perfect. How can this fact be accounted for, except on the supposition, that every such judgment is based upon a comparison of the external object, with an idea more perfect, existing, in the mind itself?

Again, the ancient sculptors and painters, when they attempted to give to the world, what all men would alike regard as the forms of perfect beauty, copied after no one living model; but took from all the forms of beauty in the world around them, those parts which were most beautiful, and from these combined new forms more beautiful than any realities actually existing. Does not this show, that they were endeavoring to realize, not the forms of beauty actually existing in the universe around them, but an idea in their own minds more perfect than these forms?

With this supposition also, and with this only, consists the fact, that the pleasure derived from the contemplation of certain forms of beauty is permanent, and becomes more intense, the more intimate and protracted our acquaintance with them; while the pleasure derived from the contemplation of other forms ceases on a protracted and intimate acquaintance. The reason of this obviously is, that the first-mentioned forms correspond very nearly, in all their arts, to the ideal in the mind. An intimate acquaintance with the others, however, gives us a knowledge of their defects, and in time destroys the pleasure which we felt when those defects were not perceived.

I will present one other consideration bearing upon the subject, which I regard as perfectly decisive. The particular elements which mark objects as beautiful or sublime, do in fact correspond with fundamental ideas. In respect to the sublime, all agree in fixing upon the infinite as the chief source of emotions of sublimity. In finite objects one element only is correlated to these emotions, that of vastness.

The characteristics of the beautiful are determinate form, regularity, uniformity, and variety. A waving, instead of a crooked line, a line realizing the ideas of uniformity and variety, has universally been fixed upon, as the line of beauty and grace. Now that which proceeds according to fundamental ideas, must be itself the representative of such ideas.

OBJECTION TO THE UNIVERSALITY OF THESE IDEAS.

An objection to the principle above elucidated, to wit, the different standards of beauty adopted by different nations, and by the same nations, at different periods, has sometimes been adduced. In reply, the following considerations are presented as deserving special attention:

1. It may be questioned whether the savage when he paints and tattoos his form, and the civilized person when he adorns his with the ornaments of civilized society, are endeavoring to realize the same idea. The one may be aiming to realize the idea of the beautiful, and the other (the savage), that of the terrible. The same holds true of architecture. The prominent idea in the Grecian style is the beautiful. That in the Gothic is the grand, the solemn, the sublime. The former and the latter then, had not different standards of beauty. They were aiming to realize different ideas.

2. While the idea may exist alike in all minds, the ideal, that is, the form in which the idea shall be embodied, may exist in different minds, and among mankind at different periods, in different degrees of development. Consequently the forms in which they will embody the idea will be various.

3. In contemplating particular forms of beauty, in which many defects of course exist along with the beautiful, these may be mistaken for the particular features which are the source of the pleasurable emotions felt under these circumstances. These defects then will be copied instead of the actual beauties.

4. But in the midst of all this apparent variety, there is a more general agreement than is commonly supposed; an agreement that is fundamental to the inquiry before us. Introduce men of all ages, and of every nation into the same family, and ask them which of the children in that particular family is the most beautiful, and you will find but little diversity in their judgments, and no diversity which is not perfectly consistent with the supposition of a common ideal in their minds, while the striking coincidence in their judgments can be explained on no other supposition.

5. There are actual forms of beauty, in respect to which all men do agree. The most perfect specimens of ancient sculpture and

painting may be adduced as an illustration. Also forms of beauty in the world around us; as, the rose and the lily. Such circumstances we should find it difficult to explain on any other supposition than the one before us.

CHRONOLOGICAL ANTECEDENTS OF THESE IDEAS.

The condition of the development of the idea of beauty and of sublimity in the mind, is the perception of the elements of the beautiful and sublime in some external object. In the divine mind, these ideas, among others, existed eternally as the prototypes after which creation was formed and moulded. The human intelligence is so constituted, that, in the presence of objects in the conformation of which the divine idea is more or less nearly realized, the same idea is awakened in the mind of man. This idea then becomes the standard by which the external object is characterized as beautiful, grand, or sublime.

ILLUSTRATION FROM COUSIN.

Cousin thus beautifully explains the origin of the idea of beauty in the mind: "The idea of the beautiful is equally inherent in the mind of man, as that of the just and the good. Interrogate yourselves, when a vast and tranquil sea, when mountains of harmonious proportions, when the manly or graceful forms of men and women, are present to your view, or some trait of heroic devotion, to your recollection. Once impressed with the idea of the beautiful, man seizes, disengages, extends, develops and purifies it in his thought, and by the assistance of this idea, which external objects have suggested to him, he re-examines these same objects, and finds them inferior to the idea which they themselves have suggested."

IDEA OF HARMONY.

The remarks and illustrations above presented, pertaining to the ideas of the beautiful and sublime, are equally applicable to that of harmony. The ear trieth sounds, as the eye doth form and color. In harmony words and sound are arranged according to fundamental ideas, just as other elements are in the beautiful and sublime. That this is the true application of the subject will appear, I think, from the following considerations:

1. When highly excited by musical performances, those who attentively watch the operations of their own minds, cannot fail to notice, that under such circumstances they uniformly conceive of the same pieces as performed infinitely better; and that it is this conception which constitutes the main source of delight.

2. Persons in whose minds the principle of harmony is most fully developed, enjoy an exquisite piece of music quite as highly, when reading it alone, in the absence of all musical sounds, as when hearing it performed by the best trained choir, clearly showing that the idea in the mind far surpasses realities without.

3. Skillful performers on the organ or piano, who have lost the faculty of hearing, enjoy these instruments no less than before. I recollect to have read of a celebrated musician in Germany, who in his old age lost his hearing entirely. Yet, as his fingers would run over the keys of his piano, the instrument used being (a fact unknown to him) totally destitute of power to produce any sound whatever, he would rise in his feelings to perfect ecstasy of delight. In his own mind there was harmony deep and profound. It was harmony in idea.

4. The principles of harmony are all found to be reducible to mathematical formulas. These principles are not deduced, in the first instance, from observation, irrespective of fundamental ideas. Such ideas must first be developed, before the principles of harmony can be understood.

We are now prepared for a definition of poetry, properly so called. A mere rhythmical jingle of words at the end of lines of a given length, does not constitute poetry, according to the true signification of the term. Nor have I been satisfied with the popular definitions of the subject which I have met with. I will present, as an example, that given by Coleridge: "A poem is that species of composition which is opposed to works of science, by proposing for its immediate object pleasure, not truth; and from all other species (having this object in common with it) it is discriminated by proposing to itself such delight from the whole as is compatible with a distinct gratification from each component part." The great objection to this definition is, that many prose, as well as poetical compositions, would fall under it. I will now propose another and a different definition. Poetry, or more properly, perhaps, a poem, is the creations of the imagination embodied in language arranged in conformity to the idea of harmony. I leave the definition to speak for itself.

IDEA OF TRUTH.——IDEA DEFINED.

Another fundamental idea of reason—an idea which controls the intelligence in all its movements—is the idea of truth. The term truth may be contemplated objectively and subjectively. Objectively, it comprehends and expresses all realities, whatever they may be. Subjectively it designates an intellectual conception in harmony with the object of the conception.

CHRONOLOGICAL ANTECEDENT OF THIS IDEA.

The chronological antecedent of this idea, or the condition of its development by the reason, is the perception of phenomena, and the consequent development of the idea of substance. Then the great question, "What is truth?" becomes the leading idea in the intelligence.

THE IDEA OF LAW,——LAW DEFINED.

Among the most fundamental of all ideas of reason is that of *law.* Law, in its most general acceptation, is defined as a *rule of action,* and in thought and fact, takes on two forms,—physical or natural, and moral; the former comprising the rule, or rules, in conformity to which the physical powers in nature *do act,* and the latter those in conformity to which moral agents *are required* to act. Natural law is a rule *of* action; moral law, on the other hand, is a rule *for* action.

LAW, SUBJECTIVE AND OBJECTIVE.

Law, then, may be contemplated in two points of light,— subjective, and objective. In the first sense, it is an idea, in which powers are contemplated as arranged relatively to each other, so that their mutual action and reaction shall produce results in correspondence to a certain end, conceived of, and chosen by the mind. In the second sense, it is the existence, arrangement, and consequent action of these powers, in harmony with that idea.

CONCLUSION FROM THE ABOVE.

We come to this conclusion: that whenever powers act in conformity with law,—powers whose arrangements take form in time, they are acting in obedience to some idea existing in some intelligent mind. To illustrate this, let us suppose an army of one hundred thousand men all dressed and equipped alike, arranged in a given order, and all performing perfectly harmonious motions and evolutions. You here perceive the presence and all-prevading influence of law. Is it possible to conceive all this, and not suppose this law to be some idea in some intelligent mind—a mind that comprehends all the parts, and assigns to each part its position, etc.? If this could not be supposed of intelligent powers much less could we suppose a similar action of necessary and unintelligent ones. The grand problem, then, the solution of which is the final object and distinctive character of philosophy, when once solved, leads the mind to the direct apprehension and contemplation of the infinite,—of God, whose creative idea is the law of all existences. The problem referred to is this: "For all that exists conditionally (*i.e.* the existence of which is inconceivable except under the condition of its dependency on some other as its antecedent) to find a ground that is unconditional and absolute, and thereby to reduce the aggregate of human knowledge to a system." Now, this ground can be found in nothing but in the mind of God.

CHRONOLOGICAL ANTECEDENT TO THIS IDEA.

As mind wakes into conscious existence, and contemplates the action of the powers of nature within and around it, it at once perceives all things existing and acting as a means to an end. Everywhere diversity blended with harmony, presents itself. Now this presentation of the powers of nature is the chronological antecedent of the idea of law in the reason. Hence the great inquiry ever after imposed upon the intelligence; to wit, What are the laws in conformity to which they act? In this inquiry, the intelligence begins to "feel after" the infinite, and it never rests until it finds itself in the presence of "that creative idea, which appoints to each thing its position, and in consequence of that position, gives it its qualities, yea, its very existence as that particular thing."

NATURE OF PROOF.

One thought suggested by the preceding analysis demands special attention,—the nature of proof. No proposition is, properly speaking, proved, till facts or arguments are adduced, which not only affirm its truth, but contradict every opposite proposition. How often is this fundamental law of evidence overlooked and disregarded in almost every department of human investigation! In theology, for example, how often is an hypothesis denominated a doctrine, which merely consists with a given class of passages of Holy Writ,—assumed as absolutely affirmed by these passages, when, in reality, they equally consist with the contradictory hypothesis! Let it ever be borne in mind, that no passage or passages of Scripture prove any one doctrine which do not contradict every opposite doctrine. No facts affirm any one hypothesis which do not equally contradict every contradictory hypothesis.

FUNDAMENTAL AND SUPERFICIAL THINKERS.

Another suggestion which presents itself is this,—the difference between superficial and fundamental thinkers. The former dwell only upon the surface of subjects, and having there found certain hypotheses which consist with mere exterior facts, they gravely decide that they "have heard the conclusion of the whole matter." They have discovered all that can be known, and "wisdom will die with them." The latter class, on the other hand, retire into the interior of subjects, and taking their position upon some great central facts, announce the existence and operations of universal laws, sustaining to exterior facts the relation of logical antecedents, and explaining them all. The reason why the positions assumed by such men are uniformly so impregnable is, that the error of every hypothesis in opposition to that which they have assumed, as well as the truth of their own, becomes visible at once, in the light of the great central facts on which they have taken their stand.

THE PHILOSOPHIC IDEA.

The philosophic idea realized, or objectively considered, is the reduction of phenomena to fundamental ideas,—the reduction of the sum of human knowledge to a system; the finding, and the infinity of facts which are floating in the universe around us, some great central fundamental facts or laws, which are affirmed by all others, and explain them all.

This idea subjectively considered is a conception lying down in the depths of the reason, that all substances exist and act in harmony with such ideas. Hence the questions perpetually imposed upon the understanding and judgment, in all departments of human research; to wit, what are the laws which explain the facts here presented? Science is everywhere now on the high road tending to the realization of this great idea. Happy the eyes that shall be realized.

IDEA OF SCIENCE DEFINED.

The idea of science, which of course is a pure conception of reason, is knowledge reduced to fundamental ideas and principles; or the properties and relations of objects, systematically evolved in the light of such ideas and principles. Thus in geometry, we have the properties and relations of particular objects systematically evolved in the light of axioms and postulates, which are, in reality, fundamental ideas of reason. Whenever this end is accomplished, in reference to any phenomena, or objects, then we have the scientific idea realized.

PURE SCIENCES.

When the axioms, postulates, and definitions are all alike pure conceptions of reason, and when the judgment evolves the properties and relations of the objects of such definitions in the light of such axioms and postulates, then we have what are denominated pure sciences. Such is geometry, and the mathematics generally.

MIXED SCIENCES.

When the axioms and postulates are ideas or principles of reason, and when the definitions pertain to phenomena or objects contingent and relative, as in natural philosophy, and when the judgment evolves the relations and properties of such objects in the light of such ideas and postulates, then we have mixed sciences.

CONSCIENCE DEFINED.

Conscience is that function of reason which pertains to the ideas of right and wrong, of obligation, of merit and demerit, etc. It is a testifying function of reason, pertaining to the relation which ought to exist between the action of the will and the idea of right and wrong.

AUTHORITY OF CONSCIENCE.

1. Conscience always commands us in the name of God. Her mandates are regarded as the voice of God speaking within us, and when disregarded, we always hold ourselves amenable to the divine tribunal. Conscience in the heathen is not only a law, but a law of God; and so it is regarded by them.

2. As conscience is the voice of God within us, it follows that it can never, in its appropriate exercise, put right for wrong, and the opposite. In other words, no man acts conscientiously when wittingly doing wrong, nor in opposition to conscience, when wittingly doing right. "Conscience," as Coleridge remarks, "in the absence of direct inspiration, bears the same relation to the will of God, that a chronometer does to the position of the sun in a cloudy day."

OBJECTION.

In opposition to the principle above stated, it is very common to refer to the contradictory standards of moral obligation adopted by different nations, communities, and individuals. The following considerations are deserving of special attention in reply to this objection:

1. To suppose that the heathen, for example, in all their rights and ceremonies, are endeavoring to realize the idea of right, is as absurd as to suppose that the savage is endeavoring to realize the idea of the beautiful, when he is tattooing his body.

2. The Bible affirms that the heathen are actuated by fear and not by conscience: "And deliver them who through fear of death were all their lifetime subject to bondage."

3. The judgment that a thing is not wrong, is often mistaken for the testimony of conscience to its rightness.

4. When a reference is made to the intention, the only appropriate object of conscience, we find a more universal agreement among men than is generally supposed, an agreement of such a nature as to demand the truth of the above proposition, while every shade of difference may be explained in perfect consistency with it.

TERM CONSCIENCE AS USED IN THE SCRIPTURES.

A good conscience, as the words are there used, is the testimony of the mind to the agreement of the will, or moral action, with the moral law. An evil conscience is the opposite, the testimony of the mind to the fact of the disagreement of the action of the will with that law.

RELATION OF REASON TO OTHER INTELLECTUAL FACULTIES.

The relation of reason to other functions of the intelligence may now be readily pointed out. Of the phenomena, or truths affirmed by those faculties, reason gives the logical antecedents. This is its exclusive function. The judgment, in all its operations, is exclusively analytic. It simply evolves what is embraced in the affirmations of the other faculties. Reason is synthetic. It always adds to the affirmation of the other faculties something not embraced in the affirmation. The element added, however, always sustains to that to which it is added a fixed relation, that of logical antecedent. Thus when sense or consciousness affirms phenomena, reason adds to the affirmation an element not embrace in it, that of substance, an element, however, staining to the affirmation a fixed relation, that of logical antecedent.

REASON COMMON TO ALL MEN.

Reason also exists in all men, and equally in all who posses it at all. This is evident from the fact that if an individual knows a truth of reason at all, he does and must know it absolutely. There are no degrees in such knowledge. The difference, and only difference, between men lies in their perceptive and reflective faculties. Newton differed from other men not because he knew, any more absolutely than they, that events suppose a cause, that things equal to the same thing are equal to one another, etc., but because he possessed powers of perception and reflection which enabled him to see (what they could not discover) the qualities involved in such truths.

CHAPTER XII.

LAWS OF INVESTIGATION.

INVESTIGATION AND REASONING DISTINGUISHED.

One department of inquiry of great importance still remains. When we have done with this, our inquiry in regard to the intellectual powers will have closed, except as far as we may find their operations combined with that of the other faculties or susceptibilities of the mind.

The department to which I refer, is the employment of these powers in what is called a process of investigation and reasoning. These processes, though intimately connected, are entirely distinct, and should be carefully distinguished the one from the other. In the former process our exclusive object is the discovery of truth. In the latter, the object equally exclusive is, to prove the truth already discovered.

Your attention in the present chapter will be directed to the first process. Our inquiry is, What are the laws which govern the mind, or ought to govern the mind, in a process of investigation of truth?

SUBSTANCES, HOW KNOWN.

All substances are revealed to us by their respective phenomena. Their existence, not only, but their nature, character and powers, are revealed to us in this manner, and this manner exclusively The induction of phenomena therefore lies at the basis of all our investigations pertaining to substances.

INDUCTION OF PHENOMENA, FOR WHAT PURPOSES MADE.

There are four purposes entirely distinct, for which an induction of phenomena is made:

1. For the purpose of discovering the nature, characteristics, and powers of some particular substance.

155

2. For the purpose of classification, into genera and species.

3. For the purpose of discovering some general fact, or order of sequence.

4. For the purpose of discovering universal laws, in conformity to which the action of substances is subordinated.

Now the principles which should guide us in the induction of phenomena depend upon the objective we have in view in such induction.

INDUCTION PERTAINING TO PARTICULAR SUBSTANCES.

In the induction of phenomena for the purposes of determining the characteristics and powers of some particular substance, the following principles are of fundamental importance in guiding our investigations.

1. In marking the phenomena which appear, or the characteristics of particular phenomena, omit none which do exist, and suppose none which do not exist.

2. In determining the particular powers of the substance in the light of phenomena thus classified and characterized, undeviatingly adhere to the following principles. Phenomena which are in their fundamental characteristics alike, suppose similar powers. Phenomena which are in their fundamental characteristics unlike, suppose dissimilar powers. In strict conformity to those principles, an attempt has been made, in a preceding part of the present treatise, to determine, among other things, the different functions of the human intelligence. Whether the effort has been successful, time will determine.

INDUCTION FOR PURPOSES OF CLASSIFICATION INTO GENERA AND SPECIES.

In the induction of phenomena for the purposes of classification into genera and species, the following principles should be strictly adhered to:

1. Fix definitely and distinctly upon the *principle* of classification, whatever it may be.

2. With a rigid regard to principle, range with the given class every object, whatever its diversities in other respects, which bears the characteristic mark.

3. Strictly exclude from the class every individual in which the characteristic mark is wanting.

The correctness and apparently easy application of the above principles are so obvious, that it would seem, that every one would find it very easy to apply them in all cases. But their rigid application, in cases where it is often most demanded, requires an intellectual integrity, and sternness of virtue, which the mass of mankind "very little wot of." Every one almost would readily apply them to shells, and rocks, and earths, and beasts, and fowls, and fishes, and even to the objects in the firmament above us. But let us suppose that an individual has before him a correct definition of treason, murder, theft, and of kindred crimes punishable by the law, and that he should discover upon an only son, a dark spot, which, if carefully examined, would mark him as a subject of one of the crimes above named; it would require the stern virtue of a Brutus, to be willing to have inquisition made according to the principles of immutable justice. Cases which thus try the virtue of mankind are of very frequent occurrence.

FINDING A GENERAL FACT, OR ORDER OF SEQUENCE.

A general fact, as we have seen, is a quality which attaches itself to each individual of a given class. Sometimes it may be peculiar to this one class; sometimes it may be common to it and other classes. In other instances, it may be an essential quality of one class, and a mere accident in connection with another. When we have ascertained a fact to be general, if an individual of a given class appears, we know, without particular investigation, that the quality is also present. In determining the question whether a fact is strictly general, the only difficulty which presents itself, is in distinguishing between an essential and an accidental quality. These two principles should determine our conclusions under such circumstances:

1. The existence or absence of perfect uniformity of experience.

2. Experience in such decisive circumstances, as to render it certain, that the fact is, or is not, an essential, and not an accidental quality of the class. Nothing but good judgment can enable one to distinguish between decisive and indecisive facts under such circumstances.

One of the most fruitful sources of error is based upon uniformity of experience in certain circumstances. The absence of such uniformity is certain evidence, that a fact has an accidental, and not a necessary connection with a certain class. Its presence, however, may constitute no certain ground for the opposite conclusion. The king of Japan, for example, reasoned very inconclusively, from an experience perfectly unvarying in his circumstances, to the conclusion, that water never, under any circumstances, exists in any other than the fluid state. To separate the decisive from the indecisive, and rest our conclusions upon the former class of facts only, is the distinguishing characteristic of strong perceptive powers associated with good judgment.

THE PROBABLE AND IMPROBABLE.

Between the perfectly certain and uncertain lie the probable and improbable. If, as has been already said, a fact has been ascertained to have a necessary connection with a given class, its presence, when any individual of the class is met with, becomes perfectly certain. But if its connection is accidental, its existence in connection with a particular individual of the class becomes probable or improbable in proportion to the uniformity or want of uniformity of experience under similar circumstances. Many of the most serious transactions of life rest upon a calculation of probabilities.

ORDER OF SEQUENCE.

The object of investigation here is to ascertain, in reference to given effects, those things which sustain to such effects the relation of real causes. The difficulty to be overcome, often consists in this. The real cause of a given effect may exist in connection with such combinations of powers, that it may be difficult if not impossible for the beholder to determine which produced it. Under such circumstances, careful experiments, in connection with close observation, can alone determine the real order of sequence. There are four important principles which should be strictly adhered to, as tests of all our conclusions in relation to such investigations:

1. When in each experiment, the combination has been different, with this exception, that one element has been present in all, and the given effect has in each instance arisen, we then conclude that this element is the real cause of the effect.

2. When, on the removal of a certain element, the given effect disappears, while it remains, this being present, when each of the others is removed, we then conclude, that this particular element is the particular cause.

3. When the given effect is the invariable consequent of the addition of a new element to a given combination, while the effect does not appear when this antecedent is not added, we then fix upon this particular antecedent as the real cause.

4. When a number of consequents exist in connection with a number of antecedents, and when a particular consequent invariably disappears on the removal of a given antecedent, we fix upon the latter as the real cause of the former.

THE DISCOVERY OF UNIVERSAL LAW.

In the induction of phenomena for the discovery of universal law, three important principles are to be strictly adhered to.

1. The phenomena must not merely consist with this particular hypothesis, but demand it as their logical antecedent.

2. Consequently such phenomena must contradict, with equal positiveness, every other contradictory hypothesis.

3. All phenomena to which the given hypothesis does not sustain the relations of logical antecedent, must be left wholly out of the account, as having no bearing upon the subject.

But this subject has been so fully treated of in the preceding chapter, that nothing further upon it is demanded here.

TESTIMONY.

It often happens, and that in reference to subjects of the greatest importance, that the facts which constitute the basis of our inquiries after truth, have never been given to us as objects of sense or consciousness. We are compelled to receive or reject them on the testimony of others. From this source, the greatest part of our knowledge, and of the most important of our knowledge, is derived.

The great inquiry here presents itself: What are the laws of evidence under the influence of which we judge ourselves bound to receive and act upon the phenomena revealed to us through the affirmations of other minds? Testimony is used for the same purpose that the faculties of sense and consciousness are used; to wit, for the ascertainment of facts, or phenomena, which constitute the basis of judgment in regard to a given subject.

CHARACTERISTICS OF THE STATEMENTS MADE BY A WITNESS.

The statements made by a witness may be contemplated in three points of light.

1. In the light of the idea of possibility or impossibility. If an individual should affirm that an idiot, remaining such, had given a scientific demonstration of some of the most abstruse problems in the higher mathematics, we should give no credit at all to his statement, on the ground of a perceived impossibility of the occurrence of such a fact. If, on the other hand, the witness should affirm that an individual remaining an idiot up to a certain period, did, from that period, manifest a high degree of mental energy, we should pronounce the statement highly improbable, though not absolutely impossible in itself. The statement, therefore, is capable of being established by testimony.

2. The statement may also be contemplated in reference to the question whether in itself, aside from the character of the witness, it is credible or incredible. A statement characterized as impossible, is absolutely incredible. No weight of testimony can render it worthy of belief. An event also may be contemplated as possible, and yet the statement that it has actually occurred may be almost wholly wanting in respect to credibility. If it should be said that a pure spirit before the throne had, without any form of temptation from without or within, violated his duty to his God, we should hesitate to pronounce the occurrence impossible in itself. Yet we

160

should deem it hardly credible. A statement, to be credible, must assert what is in itself perceived to be possible. It must also fall within the analogy of experience. Thus, to the great mass of mankind, there is wanting entirely any experience of a direct revelation from God. Yet the existence of such a revelation for the good of the race, is analogous to what all have experienced of the divine beneficence to man. There is, therefore, nothing incredible in the statement, that such a revelation has been made. A statement, then, which affirms the occurrence of an event in itself possible, and which falls within the analogy of experience, is capable of being rendered worthy of all confidence by testimony.

3. A statement is in itself probable or improbable, when it does or does not accord with general experience in similar circumstances. A thing may be possible, and, at the same time, very improbable. No one would say that is absolutely impossible that a die, when thrown, should fall twenty times in succession with the same number uppermost. Yet all would pronounce such an occurrence in an extreme degree improbable. An improbable event may be rendered worthy of belief by testimony. A much higher degree, however, is demanded to establish such an occurrence, than one which accords with what we have had experience of in similar circumstances.

CIRCUMSTANCES WHICH GO TO ESTABLISH THE CREDIBILITY OF A WITNESS.

We will now consider the circumstances which go to establish the credibility of a witness. Among them, I will specify the following, without enlarging upon any of them.

1. The most important characteristic is a character for veracity.

2. The next is a capacity to comprehend the particular facts to which he bears testimony.

3. Full opportunity to observe the facts, together with evidence that adequate attention was given to them at the time.

4. Evidence that the occurrence was of such a nature that the individual was not deceived at the time, and that it sustains such a relation to the individual, as to preclude the reasonable apprehension that his memory has failed him in respect to it.

5. An entire consistency between the statements of the witness and his conduct in respect to the events, the occurrence of which he affirms. If an individual affirms his entire confidence in the veracity of a certain person, and his entire treatment of him is in full harmony with his statements, we are bound to admit the truth of what the witness testifies in relation to his own convictions.

CORROBORATING CIRCUMSTANCES ASIDE FROM THE CHARACTER OF THE WITNESS.

But there are circumstances often attending the testimony of a witness, totally disconnected with the question of his veracity, which demand our confidence. Among these, I specify the following:

1. The entire absence of all motives to give false testimony. This principle is based upon the assumption, that men do not act without some motive, and that consequently they will not ordinarily violate the principles of truth without some temptation to do it.

2. When no assignable motives exist to induce an individual to make a given statement, if he is not convinced of its truth, and when strong motives impel him to deny it, especially if it is false, then we recognize ourselves as obligated to believe his statements without reference to his moral character at all.

3. Another circumstance which tends strongly to corroborate the statements of a witness is this: When the facts affirmed lie along the line of our own experience in similar circumstances. This, however, is not a safe principle to rely upon, in the absence of other circumstances of strong corroboration. Villains often throw their statements into harmony with experience, for the purpose of covering their dark designs.

4. When, though new, they accord with the known powers of the agent to whom they are ascribed.

5. When these facts stand connected with the development of laws and properties in the agent, before unknown.

Under such circumstances, the further removed from experience the facts are, the greater the probability of their being true, because of the greater probability that they would, if not true, have been unknown to the witness.

CONCURRENT TESTIMONY.

The confidence which we repose in the affirmations of a witness is greatly strengthened by the concurrent testimony of other individuals. Here the following circumstances should be especially taken into the account:

1. When each witness possesses all the marks of credibility above referred to.

2. When there is an entire concurrence in their statements, or a concurrence in respect to all material facts.

3. When the characters of the several witnesses are widely different,—as friends and enemies, etc., who of course must be influenced by widely different motives, and even by those directly the opposite; especially when their characters, motives, and relations to the subject are so different as to preclude the supposition of a collusion between the witnesses.

4. When one witness states facts omitted by others, and when all the statements together make up a complete account of the whole transaction.

5. When there are apparent contradictions between the statements of the witnesses, which a more enlarged acquaintance with the whole subject fully reconciles. Such occurrences in testimony preclude the supposition of collusion, and present each individual as an independent, honest witness in the case.

6. Coincidences often occur in the statements of witnesses which, from the nature of the case, are manifestly designed. When such occurrences attend the testimony of various individuals, all affirming the same great leading facts, they tend strongly to confirm the testimony given. This principle is most beautifully illustrated by Dr. Paley, in his Horae Paulinae:—a work deserving more attention than almost anything else which the Doctor ever wrote.

Great care and sound judgment are requisite in the application of the principles above stated. When they are fulfilled in the case of testimony pertaining to any subject, it would be the height of presumption and moral depravity in us not to act upon it as true. Infinite interests may be safely based upon the validity of such testimony. We are often necessitated to decide and act, however, in the absence of testimony thus full and complete, and often upon testimony failing, in many respects, of the marks of credibility above laid down. To discern between the valid and the invalid, to determine correctly when to trust and when to withhold confidence, requires stern integrity of heart, and a judgment, "by reason of use exercised," to distinguish the true from the false.

CHAPTER XIII.

THE INTELLIGENCE OF MAN AS DISTINGUISHED FROM THAT OF THE BRUTE.

It has been very common with philosophers to represent all created existences, from the highest intelligences in heaven to the crude forms of matter, as successive links in one great chain, each link in the chain, commencing with the lowest, differing mainly in degree from that which immediately succeeds it. The highest forms of brute, and the lowest of rational intelligence, for example, differ, it is asserted, not in kind, but only in degree. Of late, the reality of orders of existences, as successive links of a great chain, has come to be seriously doubted. The intelligence of man and of the brute, it is said, differs not in degree, but in kind. If we conceive of the highest forms of brute intelligence increased to any degree whatever, as far as degree is concerned, still it makes no approach at all to real rationality. The different orders of brute instincts do constitute, it is thought, different links of one chain. Those of rational intelligence constitute another and totally different chain, a chain none of the links of which are connected, in any form, with any of those of the other. This last is the opinion entertained by the author of this treatise. I will now proceed to state the grounds of this opinion.

PRINCIPLE ON WHICH THE ARGUMENT IS BASED.

In conducting our inquiries on this subject, the first thing to be settled is, the principle on which our conclusions shall be based. On all hands it is agreed, that there are points of resemblance between the manifestations of intelligence in the brute and among mankind. At the same time, there are points of dissimilarity equally manifest and important. Now let A represent the mental phenomena which appear in man, and never appear in the brute. If we can find the power or powers in man from which the phenomena represented by A result, we have then determined fully the faculties which man possesses and the brute wants. The faculties thus asserted of man, are to be wholly denied of the brute, and all the manifestations of brute intelligence are to be accounted for by a reference to what remains, after the former have been subtracted. All must admit, that this is the true and the only true principle to be applied in the case. It now remains to apply the principle to the solution of the question before us.

POINTS OF RESEMBLANCE BETWEEN THE MAN AND THE BRUTE.

That brutes, such as are supposed in the present argument, possess the faculty of external perception, such as sight, hearing, taste, smell, and touch; that such perceptions are followed by feelings of a given character, and that these feelings are followed by external actions which are correlated to the perceptions referred to, and that all these manifestations are common to man and the brute both, will be denied by none who have, however carelessly, observed the facts which have presented themselves to his notice. Such are the phenomena common to man and the brute.

HYPOTHESES ON WHICH THESE COMMON FACTS MAY BE EXPLAINED.

There are two distinct and opposite hypotheses on which these common facts may be explained. When man has an external perception, reason at once suggests certain fundamental ideas in the light of which he explains to himself the phenomena perceived, and passes certain judgments upon them. Action with him has special reference not to the phenomena, but to the judgments thus passed. All these things we know from consciousness, to be true, in reference to man.

As far as the facts under consideration are concerned, it may be that the same is true of the brute. All the phenomena of brute action, however, are equally explicable, on an entirely different hypothesis. When a brute has a perception of some object, without the presence of any fundamental ideas in the light of which he can explain to himself what he sees, and consequently form notions and judgments of the object perceived, and act in view of judgments thus formed, it may be, that such perceptions are followed

166

by certain feelings, and that from these, as necessary consequents, external acts, such as the brute puts forth, arise. All that would be intellectual with the brute, on this hypothesis, would be the simple power to *perceive* the thing, without the capacity to recognize either himself as the *subject,* or the thing perceived, as the *object,* of the perception, so as to form any conceptions or judgments pertaining either to the subject or object. The feelings which attend such perceptions, together with such as arise from the internal organism of the brute, such as hunger and thirst, are followed necessarily by external actions in harmony with the sphere for which the creature was designed. The action of the brute would be in fixed harmony with the law,—a law, however, which has no subjective existence in the intelligence of the creature, but which exists as an idea in that of the Creator. Action, in such a case, would be purely mechanical, the propelling force being the *feelings* generated as above supposed, while the law of action would be an idea which the subject of the action never apprehended, but in conformity to which the organism of the brute is formed.

A case stated in the public prints, a case, whether true or false, at least conceivable, and therefore proper to be used in illustration, will fully illustrate the hypotheses under consideration. A lady, some time before the birth of a child, was struck at by a rattlesnake, and barely escaped with her life. As a consequence of the fright of the mother, the child, when born, had upon parts of its body the marks of the serpent. His eyes had the fiery and vengeful appearance peculiar to the reptile. One arm, also, lay coiled upon its side in a manner perfectly serpentine. As the child grew up, and came into the presence of certain objects, despite of all efforts of his will to the contrary, his eyes would roll in their sockets, with the fiery vengeful appearance peculiar to the serpent when attacked by an enemy. At the same time, the arm referred to would strike at the object perceived, in exact conformity to the motions of the reptile in similar circumstances. In connection with the physical organization of this individual, two classes of actions, each equally conformed to ideas, appeared; the one class, however, the consequents of volition in harmony with conceptions and judgments, and the other caused by feelings generated by external perceptions.

Now, in conformity with the fact last named, we can explain all the phenomena of brute action, however intelligent in appearance. All such phenomena may be the exclusive result of the peculiar feelings and organism of the animal, in the total absence of the intelligence peculiar to man. The question is, Are there any facts peculiar to brute and human action, verifying this hypothesis? This question I will now endeavor to answer, in the light of the principle I have laid down as the basis of our conclusions on this subject.

POINTS OF DISSIMILARITY BETWEEN MAN AND THE BRUTE.

In order to test the validity of the hypothesis under consideration, we will now attend to the fundamental phenomena which distinguish man from the brute. Among these, I will specify only the following:

1. Man, from the laws of his intelligence, is a scientific being. The main direction of the human intelligence is not merely towards phenomena, but towards the scientific explanation of phenomena. This is one of the great wants of human nature, the scientific explanation of phenomena. All mankind agree in the assumption, that in the brute there is a total absence of this principle. Brute intelligence pertains exclusively to mere phenomena. The creature never seeks an explanation of what he sees. He acts from feelings generated by perceptions, without ever seeking an explanation of what he sees or feels.

2. Man, as a race, is progressive. The brute is perfectly stationary. For six thousand years, each race has been spectators of precisely the same phenomena. The commencement of observation with man, was the commencement of intellectual progress, which has been onward from generation to generation. With all his observations, the brute has never advanced a single step. He is now just where he was six thousand years ago. The beaver builds his dam, lives and dies, just as did the first that ever appeared on earth. The same is true of the action of every brute race.

3. Man is the subject of moral obligation, and consequently of moral government. In other words, man is a moral agent. All this is universally denied of the brute. He is never, except when man acts

towards him, as all acknowledge, irrationally, regarded or treated as the subject of moral obligation or of moral government. I might cite other points of dissimilarity, equally manifest, and equally fundamental. But these are sufficient for the present argument.

FACTS APPLIED.

It now remains to apply the facts above stated to the solution of the question under consideration. When we have determined the faculties necessarily supposed, as the condition of science, progress, and moral agency in man, we have determined the faculties which we are totally to deny of the brute. For it should be borne in mind, that the facts above named do not exist in one degree in man, and in a smaller degree in the brute. The difference is not that of degree, but of total dissimilarity. What various individuals of our race, in the respects under consideration, possess in different degrees, the brute totally wants. The faculties, therefore, which are to be affirmed of men as the condition and ground of these facts, are to be totally denied of the brute.

1. I ask, then, in the first place, What faculties constitute man a scientific being, those in the absence of which he cannot possess science, and in the possession of which he is of course scientific? Sense, the faculty of external perception, man, as we have seen, has in common with the brute. But this a creature may possess in any degree, and make no approach whatever to science. Other faculties in addition are supposed as the condition and ground of such developments. What, then, are these faculties? I answer, they are, of the primary faculties, reason, and self-consciousness; and of the secondary, understanding and judgment. In the absence of reason, fundamental ideas, in the light of which phenomena may be explained, are totally wanting, and consequently science becomes impossible. Without reason also self-consciousness would, properly speaking, be impossible, or if possible, absolutely useless, and therefore not supposable, as originating from perfect intelligence. Without reason too, conceptions, notions, and judgments would be absolutely impossible. Notions cannot be formed without ideas of reason, such as substance, cause, time, space, etc. Judgments, also, and consequently classification and generalization, cannot take

place without the idea of resemblance and difference. In other words, without reason, the exercise of the understanding and judgment is impossible; the existence of these faculties is therefore not to be supposed. If, then, as we are logically bound to do, we take from the brute, reason, self-consciousness, understanding, and judgment, what remains to him? Just what we have attributed to him; to wit, the power of external perception, together with corresponding feelings, and susceptibilities, and an external organism, the action of which is in necessary conformity to the feelings thus generated.

It should be borne in mind, that science in man does not depend upon the degree in which the faculties above named are possessed by him. The degree of the scientific movement will be, other things being equal, as the degree in which these powers are possessed. When they exist in any degree, there will be real science. The total absence of science in the brute, indicates most clearly a total absence of the scientific faculties,—faculties which are so connected with each other, that if one be conceived of as wanting, the others also must be.

The question, I repeat, is not whether the action of the brute is not in harmony with fundamental ideas; but whether these ideas have a subjective existence in his intelligence. The bee, for example, builds its cell in conformity to pure ideas of reason. But does it not thus build, not because it knows such ideas, but because of the peculiarity of its perceptions, sensations, and physical structure, all of which render its thus building mechanically necessary? The facts before us show clearly that it does.

2. In the next place, we will raise the inquiry, What faculties in man render him a progressive being? They are evidently the same as those which render him scientific, with the addition of the imagination. It is because that where phenomena appear, mankind are able, in the light of ideas of reason, to explain to themselves these facts, and thus find the fundamental principle involved in them, that, as a race, we are progressive. For this reason also mankind gain important knowledge from accidental experience, a fact which never appears in the brute. A man and a brute are swimming together across a river. They become exhausted, and

when about to sink, meet with something like a plank floating by. They both get on to it and are saved. The brute passes on without becoming a whit wiser from his experience. The occurrence constitutes an era in the history of the human race. Man reflects upon the occurrence, and hence arises all the wonders of ship-building and navigation. All these had their origin in accidental occurrences like that above supposed. In the knowledge obtained from occurrences similar in their nature, the art of printing, and all the results of steam-power, etc., originated. Man and the brute also hear melodious sounds. Each alike copies what he hears. On the part of man, these sounds are re-combined into strains still more melodious. Hence the science of music. The brute copies what he hears, but never, in a solitary instance, re-combines, in the least, what he hears. The mocking-bird presents a striking illustration of the truth of this statement. It will copy almost every melodious sound it ever hears. Yet it was never known to produce a single new combination of sounds. Such facts most indubitably indicate in the brute the total absence of all the faculties which lay the foundation for progress in man, the faculties of reason, self-consciousness, understanding, judgment, and the imagination. With these in any degree, creatures are in a corresponding degree progressive. Without them, whatever else they may possess, they are perfectly stationary. Nothing is more unphilosophical and illogical, than the conclusion often drawn, in the presence of progress on the one hand, and its total absence on the other, that brute instinct and human intelligence differ only in degree. How demonstrably evident is the conclusion, that they differ not in degree, but in kind.

3. In respect to the inquiry, What faculties in man exist as the condition and ground of moral agency in him? the answer is ready. They are the faculties above named, together with that of *free will*. The absence of those first named, in the case of the brute, has already been established. Shall we still attribute to him that of free will? The following considerations perfectly satisfy my own mind on this point.

(1.) The action of free will, in the absence of conceptions and judgments, is impossible. Till I have conceptions of A and B, and judge that one differs from the other, or at least, that one is not the other, I cannot choose between them. There may be selection, but not choice; nor can there be selection such as implies the action of the free will.

(2.) None of the phenomena of brute action necessarily suppose the presence of free will in the subject. All such phenomena are just as explicable on the opposite hypothesis as on this. Now a power is never to be supposed, when its presence is not affirmed by positive facts, or necessarily supposed by the known sphere of the subject. No such considerations demand the assumption of free will in the brute. Such an assumption therefore is wholly illogical.

(3.) All the phenomena of brute action clearly indicate the absence of the power under consideration. Place the brute in any circumstances whatever, and there let particular sensations be generated in him, and his action will be just as fixed and uniform, as that of any mechanical process whatever. As often as the experiment is repeated, it will invariably be attended with the same results. With such facts before us, how illogical the assumption of free will in the brute.

(4.) Such a power as that under consideration would be a totally useless appendage to the brute, contemplating him in reference to the sphere for which he is designed. When the intellectual faculties above named are denied him, what a useless appendage to the brute, and how worse than useless to man, in respect to the use to be made of the animal, would such an appendage as free will be. The creation of such a power, under such circumstances, would be a wide departure from all the manifestations of wisdom visible in all the divine works beside.

(5.) Finally, the power under consideration constitutes one of the most essential elements of the divine image in which man was created. Why should we suppose an element so fundamental in that image to exist in a creature, in whom all the other elements are totally wanting, and that without any solid basis for that conclusion?

Thus, by the most logical deductions, we have determined the powers of the brute, as distinguished from those of man. Taking from the former, what fundamental phenomena require us to do; to wit, the powers of reason, self-consciousness, understanding, judgment, imagination, and free will, we leave him with the powers of external perception, with a sensibility, and physical organization, of such a nature, that under the varied circumstances of his being, his action is in necessary harmony with the ends for which the all-wise Creator designed him. All the phenomena of brute action can be accounted for on this hypothesis, and its truth is also affirmed by fundamental phenomena. In this lower creation man stands alone. There is nothing like him "in the heavens above, nor in the earth beneath, nor in the waters under the earth." There he stands, "the image and glory of God." Fallen though he is,

> "his form has yet not lost
> All its original brightness, nor appears
> Less . . . . . than the excess
> Of glory obscured."

GENERAL REMARKS.

1. We are now prepared to explains the ground of the mis-judgment so common in respect to the action of the brute. Men judge of brute action in the light of their own consciousness, pertaining to similar actions in themselves. When men and brutes are placed in similar circumstances, and the external actions of both are similar, men often conclude that the brute acts in view of the same conceptions and judgments, in view of which they are conscious of acting themselves. Now such conclusions are wholly unauthorized. The external manifestations of instinctive and rational intelligence may be, in many important respects, similar, yet there may be a total dissimilarity in the nature of these different kinds of intelligence.

2. We are also prepared to state the conclusion which the facts connected with brute intelligence force upon us. It is one of these two: Either the intelligence of the brute is incomparably more perfect than that of man, or, aside from the power of external perception, he has no intelligence at all, such as man possesses. The first manifestations of intelligence in man, how imperfect and feeble! How rude and ill-shaped, for example, the first habitations built by man! How slow the progress of human architecture from such rude beginnings to its present perfection! On the other hand,

the first production of the brute bears the stamp of perfection. The first dam built by the beaver, the first nest built by the bird, have never been surpassed. The first cell built by the bee can hardly be improved, even in thought. Now suppose that such actions of the brute are, as is the case with man, the result of the carrying out of an idea, a plan, previously developed in his intelligence, what must we conclude? Why, that the first race of brutes that ever appeared on earth, had a degree of intelligence which man, after six thousand years of laborious progress, has hardly reached. This or the opposite one forces itself upon us.

3. Another consideration to which I would direct attention is this the facts on which the conclusions of individuals have been based, in respect to the existence of the higher powers of intelligence in the brute, as contrasted with others in the same connection, which have been totally overlooked. A distinguished naturalist, for example, states that the wild ass, when he begins to flee from a man, will first turn one ear, and then the other, backwards towards the object of his terror. From this fact, he concludes that the animal is deliberating what course he shall take; and, as a consequence, attributes to it the possession of the powers of deliberation and free will. A grave conclusion, surely, to infer from the leering of an ass, the existence of such powers. How often the actions of the elephant have been proclaimed, as proof of the existence of the high powers of intelligence in that animal! Now let us contemplate another class of facts in connection with the same animal. Those who have visited menageries are familiar with the dancing of the animal at the "sound of the lyre," actions as indicative of superior intelligence as any he ever puts forth. How was the creature taught such an act? Did he take lessons, as men do, and thus acquire it? It was by a process very different from this. When the keepers wish to have the animal acquire the art under consideration, they place him upon a floor covered with plates of iron. These plates are gradually heated till the creature, beginning to feel pain in his feet from the heat, lifts first one foot and then the other. As soon as such motions begin, the music commences, which is made to become more and more lively as the animal steps with greater and greater rapidity. When this process has been

174

continued for a sufficient length of time, the music ceases, and the animal is instantly taken from his painful condition. These experiments being repeated a few times, such an association is established been the sound of the lyre, and the sensibility of the animal that as soon as he hears the music he begins to dance, and continues the pace till the music ceases. Thus we have the elephant dancing in his wisdom, as many suppose. Now had the animal the real intelligence possessed by any individual of our race, who is in any degree removed above absolute idiocy, such an imposition could not be practiced on him for a single hour.

The actions of the creature, in this case, in conformity to intelligence, are not, as all perceive, a manifestation of intelligence in him, but in the keeper. So whatever intelligence the animal manifests in any instance, is not an indication of intelligence in him, but in the Creator. The same is true of all other animals.

4. The form in which memory exists in brutes, may now be readily pointed out. Memory, in man, is the recalling of the fact that we were, in particular circumstances, the subjects of such and such thoughts, feelings, etc. In the brute no such recollections can occur. When the brute has been affected in a given manner, in given circumstances, the same sensations are reproduced in him when he comes into similar circumstances again, and hence the same actions are repeated.

5. Finally, we notice the error of some who attempt to count for the diversities of intellectual manifestations between men and brutes, on the ground of diversities of phrenological development. To suppose that the soul of a dog, if placed in connection with the brain of a Newton, would manifest the intelligence of that great Philosopher is as illogical as to suppose that gold and water will exhibit the same phenomena, when subject to the same influences. The manifestations of substances diverse in their nature will, under the same circumstances, be as diverse as their nature. The brute, in any circumstances is still a brute, and not a man, nor angel. Diversities of Phrenological development may account for the diverse intellectual manifestations among men; but not for those between man and the brute. The brute must become another being, before he can manifest the intelligence of man.

PART II.

———

THE SENSIBILITIES.

———

CHAPTER I.

RECAPITULATION.

The general faculties of the mind we have comprehended under a threefold division. The intellect, the sensibilities and the will; the first comprehending all the phenomena of *thinking* and *knowing,* the second those of *feeling,* and the third those of *willing.* The first main division we have already considered.

THEIR DIVERSITIES AND RELATIONS.

Thought, feeling, and willing, how distinct and diverse are they, one from each of the others! Nothing but a fundamentally false philosophy can fail to discriminate between them. Though perfectly diverse in their nature and essential characteristics, however, they sustain the most obvious and important relations to each other. Neither class exists in the mind for any considerable time, without the presence of the others. Feeling awakens thought and impels to acts of willing. Thought, on the other hand, originates and intensifies feeling, and regulates the voluntary activities; while willing is governed by, or controls feeling, and conforms, or refuses to conform, to thought. As our analysis proceeds, these varied relations will be brought out distinctly before the mind. When feeling is strong and fixed by some engrossing object, then thought moves in the sublimity of power, and the will acts with corresponding steadiness and energy. When feeling is dull and sluggish, thought is indistinct and feeble, and the will seems to be smitten with a kind of paralysis. Clear and distinct thought, on the other hand, gives birth to strong and vivid emotions and desires, and steadies and energizes the action of the will, while both the other faculties may be aroused to the most vigorous exercise by self-originated acts of the faculty last named.

ORDER OF INVESTIGATION.

In pursuing our specific inquiries into this department of the mind, the following order will be observed. We shall first of all inquire into those complex states in which we find the action of sensibility associated with that of the other faculties.

GENERAL CHARACTERISTICS OF THESE PHENOMENA.

In concluding this introductory chapter, I would invite special attention to the following general characteristics of the phenomena of the sensibility:

1. The first characteristic that I notice is possessed by these phenomena in common with those of the intelligence; to wit, *necessity.* Certain conditions are necessary to the existence of the phenomena of sensibility; but when these conditions are fulfilled, the phenomena cannot but exist, with all the peculiar elements which characterize each peculiar feeling.

2. They are in their nature *transitory.* When certain conditions are fulfilled, they exist,—immediately pass through certain modifications, and then cease to be. Thus it is that a perpetual current of ever varying phenomena of this kind, is continually passing under the eye of consciousness. It may be questioned whether one identical feeling, unmodified, ever re-appears upon the theatre of consciousness. The only apparent exception to the above remark is found in certain feelings, to be designated hereafter, such as remorse, etc.

3. No two feelings can exist together in the mind without one entirely annihilating the other, or each so modifying the other that an entire new state of feeling is induced, with characteristics essentially different from either. Often, for example, the most deadly hate is totally annihilated by the overpowering influence of pain, fear, or personal interest. Often the abhorrence of crime is greatly

modified, if not annihilated, by the strong action of parental, filial, or conjugal affection.

4. All the phenomena of the sensibility, with one exception, to be mentioned hereafter, sustains to the will the relation of a principle of action, impelling the will to seek or avoid the object of that feeling. Hunger, thirst, pity, love, fear, etc., each impels the will to seek or avoid its own object. Two or more of these feelings often co-exist, sometimes impelling in the same, but often in different directions. Hence, the will is frequently necessitated to gratify one feeling in opposition to the impulse of another. This leads us to notice another important characteristic of these phenomena, which is,

5. The fact that every susceptibility, or rather the action of every susceptibility, impels the mind to seek *unlimited* gratification: and that in opposition to every other impulse. The feeling of hunger, thirst, fear, love, or hatred,—as long as it exists at all,—impels the will towards its own exclusive object, irrespective of every other impulse. Hence the will, by an unlimited obedience to some one impulse, often wrecks the entire system of the individual.

6. The phenomena of the sensibility are in themselves destitute of the *moral* qualities. They impel the will to *choices* which do possess a moral character. For the moral quality is to be found in the choice and not in the impulse. We might with the same propriety be called to an account for the peculiar sensations produced by the action of heat upon the human system, as for any other phenomena resulting from the direct and immediate action of the original susceptibilities of our nature. The acts of the will, associated with the phenomena of the sensibility, constitute a complex state of mind, which the conscience characterizes as right and wrong. Nothing can be more destructive of the entire system of moral obligation, than the theory of Dr. Brown, Payne, and others, which presents to our contemplation certain phenomena of the sensibility as "involving no moral feelings," and others as involving such feelings; while each is represented as the direct and necessary result of the action of the original susceptibilities of our nature. We might with the same propriety search for virtue in the sunshine or vernal showers, or for vice in the whirlwind, as in

the immediate and necessary phenomena of the Sensibility. In all these phenomena, aside from the controlling influence of the will, man is a mere passive recipient of an extraneous influence, exerted without his choice, and totally independent of his control.

IMPORTANCE OF THIS SUBJECT.

The following extract from the writings of Dr. Thomas Brown will set distinctly before the mind the importance of our present inquiries. "We might perhaps," he says, "have been so constituted, with respect to our intellectual states, as to have had all the varieties of these, our remembrances, judgments, and creations of fancy, without our emotions. But without emotions which accompany them, of how little value would the mere intellectual functions have been! It is to our vivid feelings of this class we must look for those tender regards which make our remembrances sacred, for that love of truth, of glory, and of mankind, without which to animate and reward us, in our discovery and diffusion of knowledge, the continued exercise of judgment would be a fatigue rather than a satisfaction, amid all that delightful wonder which we feel when we contemplate the admirable creations of fancy, or the more admirable beauties of the unfading model,—that model which is ever before us, and the imitation of which as has been truly said, is the only *imitation* that is itself *originality*. By our other mental functions we are mere spectators of the machinery of the universe; living in and animated by our emotions we are admirers of nature, lovers of men, adorers of God."

Nor is the importance of our present inquiries set forth with less vividness, by the less attractive aspects of the subject, as presented by our author. "In this picture of our emotions, however," he adds, "I have presented them" in their fairest aspects; there are aspects which they assume, as terrible as these are attractive; but even terrible as they are, they are not the less interesting objects of our contemplation. They are the enemies with which our mortal combat, in the warfare of life is to be carried on; and of those enemies that are to assail us, it is good for us to know all the misery which would await our defeat, as well as all the happiness which would crown our success, that our conflict may be the stronger, and our victory therefore the more sure. In the list of our emotions of this formidable class, is to be found every passion which can render life guilty and miserable; a single hour of which, if that hour be an hour of uncontrolled dominion may destroy happiness forever and leave little more of virtue than is necessary for giving all its horror to remorse. There are feelings as blasting to every desire of good that may still linger in the heart of the frail victim who is not yet wholly corrupted, as those pernicious gales of the desert, which not merely lift in whirlwinds the sands that have often been tossed before, but wither even the few fresh leaves which, on some spot of scanty verdure, have still been flourishing amid the general sterility."

CHAPTER II.

PHENOMENA OF THE SENSIBILITY CLASSIFIED.

Mental philosophers differ not a little in their classification of sensitive phenomena. Dr. Brown, for example, classifies all such phenomena with reference to the idea of *time,* as immediate, retrospective, and prospective. Prof. Upham divides these phenomena as natural and moral, while Dr. Hickok makes three classes, the animal, rational, and spiritual. Prof. Haven, on the other hand classifies the sensibilities as *simple emotions, affections,* and *desires.* One general objection holds against these and all other similar forms of classification. They are incomplete, sensations and appetites being omitted. This holds strictly with respect to all the forms above given, Dr. Hickok's excepted, and the discrimination which he has made between rational and spiritual emotions is in reality, a distinction without a difference, spiritual emotions and propensities pertaining as really and truly to the rational department of our nature as to any other. Similar remarks are obviously applicable to the forms of classification adopted by Dr. Reid, Mr. Dugald Stewart, and others.

We have endeavored to find a principle of classification free from all such objections,—a principle that may be readily comprehended, on the one hand, and which will, on the other, be strictly universal in its application. This principle is found in the two-fold nature of man, and in his consequent relations to the world of matter, thought, and voluntary activity. As being in the body, and through it connected with the universe of material causes we, in common with the animal creation around us, are capacitated to receive certain impressions, and are the subjects of corresponding propensities and desires. As capacitated for the functions of thinking and knowing, and as adapted, in our sensitive natures to the varied spheres and objects of thought and knowledge, we are the subjects of another and quite diverse class of sensitive states. Finally as capacitated for endlessly diversified forms of voluntary activity in the adaptation of our sensitive natures to such forms, we are endowed with certain general active principles and are the subjects of corresponding sensitive impulsions. We, therefore, present the following as the general and all-comprehending classification of the varied phenomena of the sensibility; to wit, 1. Those which pertain to us as a part of the animal creation, and which include *sensations* and the *appetites,* or *animal* propensities. 2. Those which pertain to us as rational beings, our *emotions* and *affections.* 3. Those which pertain to us, as capacitated for diversified forms of *voluntary activity,* or our general active principles and impulsions. These three classes of the sensibilities we shall treat of in the order above presented.

TERMS DEFINED. SENSATIONS, EMOTIONS, DESIRES, PROPENSITIES, APPETITES, AFFECTIONS, GENERAL ACTIVE PRINCIPLES, PASSIONS.

Before proceeding to an elucidation of the varied classes of the sensibilities, it may be important to define, specifically certain terms which will be frequently employed hereafter.

Sensations are those states of the sensibility which directly and immediately succeed any impressions, made by any cause, upon the physical organization.

Emotions, on the other hand, are those sensitive states directly and immediately induced by the presence of any *thought* in the mind.

When any states of the sensibility are excited from any cause or causes,—states impelling the mind to seek or avoid any particular object or objects, such impulsive states are denominated *desires.*

When the original constitution of our nature renders certain classes of desires habitual, or permanent, that particular department of the sensibility is called a *propensity.* Such for example are our desires for food, for drink, and our love of knowledge.

When the object of any given propensity is purely physical, such as food or drink, said propensity takes the name *appetite.*

When the object of any propensity is a living being, or a class of living beings, the propensity is then commonly denominated an *affection*. The love of kindred, for example, is called an affection.

When on the other hand the object of a given propensity is an object of pure thought, or an intellectual apprehension, said propensity is commonly designated by such terms as *principle, desire,* or *love.* Such, for example, is the principle of *curiosity,* the love of *knowledge,* or the desire for *action.* When the object of a given propensity, is some form of voluntary activity, such for example as action in conformity, or in opposition, to the law of duty, such impulsive propensities are denominated *general active principles.*

When any given propensity, I remark finally, becomes very strongly and permanently developed, and its gratification becomes a leading object of desire and pursuit, said propensity is denominated a passion. Thus individuals are said to have a passion for music, for painting, or for particular forms of activity.

CHAPTER III.

ANIMAL PHENOMENA AND PROPENSITIES.

Sensations, as we have defined them, are those states of the sensibility which directly and immediately succeed any impressions made by any cause or causes, upon the physical organization. Sensation and external perception are states of mind which commonly accompany each other, but, for that reason, are none the less distinct and separate, the one from the other, and pertain to entirely different departments of the mind. Sensation is exclusively a state of the sensibility. Perception is, as exclusively, a state of the intelligence.

Nor is sensation, in its nature, more distinct and separate from external perception than it is from all acts of internal perception, or consciousness, which always accompany this and all other states of the sensibility. In no case, do we, as some suppose, *feel* because we are conscious of the feeling. We are, on the other hand, conscious of feelings, because we do experience them. Perception, external, and internal, implies the prior existence of its object. No object, or mental state, exists because we perceive it. We perceive it, on the other hand, because it does exist.

Sensations of a certain class are induced by the action of appropriate causes upon any department of the physical organization. Others are experienced exclusively through the action of special organs. The sensations, for example, induced by mere tactual impressions, are nearly or quite identical, whatever department of the physical organization is affected. Those, on the other hand, which are induced by the action of the organs of taste, smell, and hearing, are special and peculiar; and those received through any one organ are wholly unlike those received through any other. The varied sensations of taste, we experience exclusively through one and the same organ, and how unlike are all these, to those received through the organs of smell, or hearing. Yet the *ultimate* states of mind induced by one class of sensations may be so much like those induced by another, that the objects of one may *suggest* those of the other. Hence the figurative impressions, sweet sounds, beautiful music, etc.

Sensations of all classes take rank as *pleasurable, painful,* or *indifferent.* Some have a positive character, and as such, occasion desires for the presence or absence of their respective causes. Others which are void of such characteristics, occasion no desires whatever.

When the physical organization is, throughout, in a healthy state, and each organ performs its proper functions, the mind has its continual dwelling place in the midst of forms of pleasurable sensations which impart sunlight to the countenance, sweetness to the temper, hopeful visions of the future, and cheerfulness to all states of being. In the opposite state of the physical organization and functions, in the absence of positive pain, there may be the perpetual presence of sensations which sour the temper, sadden the countenance, and impart the aspect of gloom to all objects of thought. Persons of the purest piety not unfrequently write bitter things against themselves, for no other reasons than the conscious presence of sensations thus induced, their real causes being misapprehended.

Through sensation exclusively, we attain to a knowledge of the *secondary qualities* of matter. The primary qualities, as we have seen, are to the mind, the objects of *direct* and *immediate,* or *presentative,* knowledge, and are, therefore, to be regarded as the *known* objects of *conscious* states of the *intelligence.* The secondary qualities, on the other hand, are recognized as the *unknown,* causes of *conscious* states of the *sensibility.* The great fundamental error in philosophy,—the exclusive cause of all forms of skepticism in science and religion, is the dogma, that all our knowledge of matter is through the exclusive medium of sensation, and, therefore, not valid for realities as they are in themselves.

APPETITES.

The following prominent characteristics of this class of our active principles, given by Mr. Dugald Stewart, present the subject in a very clear and definite manner to our minds.

"1. They take their rise from the body, and are common to us with the brutes.

"2. They are not constant, but occasional.

"3. They are accompanied with an uneasy sensation, which is strong or weak in proportion to the strength or weakness of the appetite." "Our appetites," he further observes, "are three in number: hunger, thirst, and the appetite of sex. Of these, two were intended for the preservation of the individual; the third, for the continuation of the species; and without them reason would have been insufficient for these important purposes. Suppose, for example, that the appetite of hunger had been no part of our constitution. Reason and experience might have satisfied us of the necessity of the use of food for our preservation; but how should we have been able, without an implanted principle, to ascertain according to the varying states of our animal economy, the proper seasons for eating, or the quantity of food that is salutary to the body."

These observations are in general so just that but few additional remarks are deemed requisite.

1. The number of our appetites as given by the author is evidently too limited. The propensity for sleep, and for muscular action, may as properly, and for the reasons stated above, be called appetites, as those already mentioned. The same general observations apply to the latter as to the former.

2. The law of our appetites, when they are directed to their appropriate ends, presents a very striking indication and illustration of the benevolence of our Creator. The law to which we refer is the *pleasure* which accompanies their indulgence, —a pleasure so great that the chief incentive to proper indulgence, is the pleasure, and not the end for which the appetite was given as a part of our nature. The child grows and increases in strength from food and exercise, in seeking which, these ends constitute no part of his motives.

3. The highest physical enjoyment through the indulgence of the appetites, is when indulgence is strictly subordinated to the laws of life and health; a fact which presents another and most striking illustration of the divine beneficence.

4. When the appetites have been properly controlled and directed to their proper objects, their demands present the proper limits to indulgence. A man, for example, whose appetite for food is in a healthy and unperverted state, and when feeding upon nature's simple elements, will find his appetite the best possible guide in regard to the quantity of food proper to be eaten.

5. A special law of our nature in regard to the indulgence of all the appetites in common, here demands particular attention. Properly regulated indulgence, while it does not increase, but rather diminishes perhaps, the power of the appetite, and the intensity of its action, tends to increase, rather than diminish, the gratification attending such indulgence. Excessive indulgence, on the other hand, perpetually increases the power of the appetites and the painful intensity of its action, while the degree of enjoyment attending indulgence perpetually diminishes, and is ultimately, almost or quite entirely lost. Hunger, for example, is by no means so painful to the temperate man as it is to the glutton, while the former finds forms and degrees of enjoyment in partaking of food to which the latter is a stranger. Enslavement under the power of appetite, also, is attended with a perpetual consciousness of criminal self-degradation not only utterly incompatible with any form or degree of mental blessedness, but which must issue in the deepest forms of mental wretchedness. Byron, for example, had sounded the depths of sensual indulgence in all its forms. What was the result, as evinced in his dark experience? Let him speak for himself.

> And dost thou ask, what secret woe
> I bear, corroding joy and youth?
> And wilt thou vainly seek to know
> A pang even thou must fail to soothe?

It is not love, it is not hate,
  Nor low ambition's honors lost,
That bids me loathe my present state,
  And flee from all I prized the most.
It is that weariness which springs
  From all I meet, or hear, or see;

To me no pleasure Beauty brings;
  Thine eyes have scarce a charm for me.
It is that settled, careless gloom
  The fabled Hebrew wanderers bore;
That will not look beyond the tomb,
  But cannot hope for rest before.
What exile from himself can flee?
  To zones, though more and more remote,
Still, still pursues, where e'er I be,
  The blight of life, the demon, thought.

Through many a clime 't is mine to go,
  With many a retrospection curst;
And all my solace is to know,
  Whate'er betides, I've known the worst.
What is that worst? nay, do not ask;—
  In pity from the search forbear.
Smile on—nor venture to unmask
  Man's heart, and view the hell that's there.

To that hell every living drunkard, glutton, and debauches is rapidly descending, if he is not already there. The individual on the other hand, who has wisely disciplined all his appetites and other propensities to a wholesome subjection to the laws and principles of health and purity, not only participates in the highest forms of physical enjoyment, but has perpetual mental blessedness in the consciousness that he really ranks among nature's noblemen.

ARTIFICIAL APPETITES.

Besides those appetites which necessarily arise from the constitution of our physical system, there are others which are induced by custom and use, and which consequently, may properly be denominated *acquired,* or *artificial.* Of this character are the appetites for the various narcotic and stimulating drugs and intoxicating drinks. The strength of such appetites is, in general, in proportion to their destructive tendencies. In reference to such propensities total abstinence is the only principle demanded by morality and prudence; for by indulgence the will power is constantly diminished, while the desire becomes more and more imperious, until voluntary power is overwhelmed in the unequal struggle and the deluded victim becomes a fettered *slave* to appetite and passion.

CHAPTER IV.

EMOTIONS.

Emotions have been defined, as those states of the sensibility which directly and immediately *succeed* the presence of any *thought* in the mind. Emotions sustain the same relations to thought, that sensations do to impressions made upon the physical organization.

EMOTIONS CLASSIFIED, AND ELUCIDATED.

All emotions are, in their nature, pleasant or unpleasant, joyful or saddening, happifying or painful, ecstatic or agonizing, and may be classified accordingly. An emotion which simply excites, without agitating the mind, is called pleasant or unpleasant, according to its nature. Those which are attended with certain degrees of agitation, are called joyful or saddening. Those which are attended with still higher degrees of excitement are denominated happifying or painful, while those which are attended with the highest degrees of agitation, are denominated triumphant, ecstatic or agonizing. Those emotions which attend the apprehension of good or ill to come, are represented by such terms as hope or fear. Those emotions which are induced by the apprehension of positive excellences, natural or moral, or their opposites, are represented by such terms as, favor or disfavor, approbation or reprobation, delight or abhorrence, love or hate, according to the character of the qualities referred to. When any form of good, once possessed or hoped for, has been lost, the painful emotions attending the apprehension of such a fact, is represented by such terms as regret, mourning, or grief. When objects of thought, present and future wear the prevailing aspect of unhopefulness, the emotions induced take on the form of gloom, or despondency. When the element of hope becomes wholly extinct, the emotions of agony then induced, are represented by such terms as misery and despair. The consciousness of

190

personal excellences or defects, is attended with emotions represented by such terms as self-congratulation and self-esteem, or self depreciation and mortification. If such excellences and defects are of a moral nature, taking on the form of conscious virtue or vice, good or ill desert, the joyful or agonizing emotions then induced are represented by such words as self-approval, and self-commendation, or self-reprobation and remorse. When joyful or regretful emotions are induced by the contemplation of good or ill enjoyed or endured by others, such emotions are denominated sympathetic. When emotions of regret are induced by the contemplation of good enjoyed, or of gratification in view of suffering endured, by others, such emotions are called malign.

CAUSES OF OUR EMOTIONS CLASSIFIED.

The objects of those thoughts which induce these diverse classes of emotions, are classed as agreeable or disagreeable, pleasant or unpleasant, beautiful or deformed, desirable or undesirable, lovely or hateful, excellent or execrable, perfect or imperfect, according to the nature and character of the feelings which they induce.

EMOTIONS AS DISTINGUISHED FROM DESIRES.

Emotions and desires have already been defined. We desire the presence or absence of objects which have previously excited in us pleasurable or painful sensations or emotions. The pleasure or pain must have pre-existed, or the existence of desire would be impossible. Desires are to sensations and emotions, what effects are to causes.

Emotions, as well as sensations, as distinguished from desires, are denominated *passive impressions.* Desire, on the other hand, is, in a certain sense, an active state, a state in which the mind is impelled to or from some object.

HAPPINESS OR MISERY CONDITIONED ON OUR SENSATIONAL AND EMOTIVE STATES.

Upon the nature and character of our sensations and emotions, our happiness or misery is conditioned. We are happy, when our passive impressions are of a pleasant, and unhappy or miserable, when they are of a painful, character. Happiness has been defined by some individuals, as gratified desire. This is a mistake. We have many desires of great strength,—desires the gratification of which affords little or no happiness. A man for example, may very strongly desire to witness the death of a friend, while the gratification of that desire, will, as he well knows, give pain instead of pleasure. The desire for revenge very strongly impels the will, while the gratification of the impulse is painful rather than otherwise. The happiness derived from gratified desire depends wholly upon the *passive impressions,* the sensations or emotions with which such gratification is attended.

IDEAS REPRESENTED BY THE TERMS,
HAPPINESS, BLESSEDNESS, MISERY, ETC.

When the mind is in a condition in which its sensitive and emotive states, in continued succession, are pleasant or unpleasant, pleasurable or painful, it is then in that state represented by the terms happiness or blessedness, unhappiness or misery, and its happiness or misery is perfect or imperfect, when one class of feelings exists without the presence of the other, or in the degree in which the two are intermingled with each other. The terms heaven and hell, as employed in the Scriptures and in common life, represent the idea of two distinct and opposite conditions of existence, the one in which all sensitive and emotive states are of an exclusively, happifying, and the other in which they are of an equally painful character. Our present condition of living is a mingled one. None are perfectly happy, and few are absolutely miserable.

TRANSIENT AND PERMANENT EMOTIONS.

In regard to our emotions, this principle generally holds true, that the same identical feeling is seldom reproduced by the reappearance of the same thought; and the repetition of that appearance is generally attended with a diminution of the vividness of the emotion. This, by no means holds true of the objects of the domestic affections, of moral and eternal truth, or of any objects having in them the elements of real, and especially of absolute, perfection. Familiarity with such objects, even when nothing new is developed, increases rather than diminishes their power over the sensibilities. Forms of perfect symmetry and beauty in nature, and in art, are, to all who have once attained to a proper appreciation of their excellences, objects of undying interest. This holds especially true of all real forms of mental and moral beauty and perfection. The main reason why other and common objects, after our first knowledge of them, lose their power over our emotions, is that familiarity renders us conscious of their defects, and therefore destroys our interest in them.

Emotions which depend upon the original principles and propensities of our nature are permanent in their characteristics, while those which depend upon accidental circumstances, on the other hand, are of transitory continuance. Those emotions, for example, which arise in connection with the domestic affections, the love of right and duty, and the hatred of wrong, etc., have permanent characteristics; while those of surprise at the appearance of objects new or strange, or in unexpected circumstances, after a short continuance, disappear forever.

GROWTH AND DECAY OF EMOTIONS.

Some emotions come to full maturity almost instantly. Of this character, for the most part, are emotions of surprise, wonder, fear, and terror; and the decay of such emotions is commonly as rapid as their growth. Other emotions come to maturity gradually, such, for example, as those awakened by the contemplation of objects intrinsically beautiful, sublime, or excellent. Emotions of this character are of slow and gradual decay, if they decay at all, while many of them are of permanent continuance, and are attended with increase rather than diminution of strength, from the lapse of time.

CONCORDANT AND DISCORDANT, SIMILAR AND DISSIMILAR.

As two or more distinct objects of thought may be before the mind at the same time, so two or more emotions may co-exist in the consciousness. Of co-existent emotions, some blend in unison, mutually inducing a new state of mind concordant with each of the blended emotions. Thus excellence of speech associated with personal charms, may blend into a common feeling of admiration for the individual in whom such excellences meet. Other emotions, while they do not thus blend, increase and intensify each other's characteristics. Of this class are love for a friend, and sorrow for his misfortunes. Such emotions do not blend, yet each intensifies the other. Emotions of the two kinds under consideration are said to be *concordant*.

Other co-existing emotions refuse to blend, as admiration for personal charms, and reprobation for crimes. Some are so incompatible with each other, that one will extinguish the other. Thus parental love often extinguishes wholly the resentment awakened by the misconduct of a child. Emotions of this class are called discordant emotions. The effect upon the mind induced by concordant emotions is, for the most part, pleasing, while that induced by discordant ones is commonly of a painful character.

Emotions, in their nature wholly unlike, may tend to induce the same *tone* of mind. Cheerful or melancholy emotions, however unlike their causes may be, are of this character, and are hence called similar emotions. Other emotions, such as those of pride and humility, gayety and gloominess, as they tend to induce opposite tones of mind, are called *dissimilar* emotions.

SYMPATHETIC AND REPELLANT EMOTIONS.

All are aware, that the contemplation of certain emotions as existing in other minds, tends to induce similar feelings in our own. We contemplate, for example, signal acts of gratitude, courage, heroism, or benevolence; as a result, emotions are induced in our minds prompting the desire to perform similar acts ourselves. The contemplation of joy or sorrow in others induces similar emotions in ourselves. Emotions thus "tending to induce similar feelings in other minds are called emotions of sympathy, or *sympathetic* emotions.

There are other emotions the contemplation of which tends to induce in our minds, feelings wholly unlike themselves. Acts of cruelty, for example, not only induce feelings of reprobation for the acts themselves, but emotions of compassion for the individuals injured. Emotions, the contemplation of which induces such effects, are called *repellant,* or unsympathetic emotions.

CONGRUOUS AND INCONGRUOUS EMOTIONS.

Emotions are often compared with their objects, or causes, and are deemed congruous when they do, and incongruous, when in kind they do not correspond, with the character of said objects. Emotions of admiration, for example, for objects really beautiful, sublime, or excellent; courage in the midst of peril, or compassion for the afflicted, we approve as suitable, fit, and proper; while feelings such as high esteem for objects low, mean, or trifling in their nature; of terror in the absence of real danger, or indifference in the presence of real suffering and want, we disapprove: as out of place, and improper. The same holds true, when the degree and intensity of the feelings do, or, do not, accord with the real merits or demerits of their objects. Emotions harmless in their nature, but, in kind or degree, the opposite of what would naturally be expected in the circumstances, excite in the spectator, the sense of the ludicrous, or ridiculous; such manifestations for example, as emotions of fear or terror when there is hardly the appearance of danger, or of pride or vanity on account of trivial excellences, or of wonder or surprise at things not new or strange. Emotions of delight in things odious or trivial move our disgust, contempt, or reprobation. Emotions of pleasure or indifference, at misfortune or suffering, and of hate of what is truly excellent and praiseworthy, as objects of thought, excite in us feelings of horror or indignation. All emotions, in short, of every kind whether of love or hate, delight or disgust, admiration or reprobation, of courage or terror, hope or despair, are to the spectator, congruous, when they are in harmony with their objects. They are incongruous when in kind or degree, this compatibility is wanting.

AGREEABLE AND DISAGREEABLE EMOTIONS.

The mind not unfrequently makes its own emotive states, as well as those of others, the objects of thought and contemplation. When thus contemplated, they become the causes of pleasant or unpleasant, pleasurable or painful emotions. Hence, as causes of agreeable, or disagreeable feelings, emotions are classed, like other objects, as agreeable or disagreeable. Almost, if not quite universally, congruous emotions, as objects of *thought,* are agreeable, and all of the incongruous ones are disagreeable to the mind; and that whether said emotions are, in themselves, pleasurable or painful. The mind is universally pleased with fitness, propriety, and congruity, and nowhere more intensely than when those ideas are fully realized in the relations between its own conscious mental states and their respective objects. In circumstances in which painful emotions, and those only, are fit and proper, the mind is pleased with their presence, and would be grieved at their conscious absence. Here we have the explanation of what is called "pleasure in tragic scenes." The emotions immediately excited by such scenes are exclusively painful; as objects of *thought,* however, such emotions are agreeable, being to the mind conscious indications of the right state of the sensibilities.

CHAPTER V.

MENTAL PROPENSITIES.

THE AFFECTIONS.

The propensities have been defined, as those original principles or laws of our sensitive nature which render certain classes of desires habitual or permanent in our experience. When the object of such propensity is a living being, or a class of living beings, said principle of our nature, is denominated an affection. The object of this chapter is to classify this division of mental phenomena, and give their essential characteristics. In this class of the propensities we enumerate the following:—the love of *society*, the love of *kindred*, the love of the *sexes*, the love of *friends*, the love of *home*, the love of *country*, the love of *benefactors*, the love of the *species*, the love of *God*. We shall consider these in the order above specified.

THE LOVE OF SOCIETY.

From the original constitution of our nature, we are social beings. Society, of some sort, is so essential to our well-being that absolute solitude is intolerable. When excluded from human society, association with the irrational creation is sought as a necessary alleviation of that sense of utter desolation which, if long continued, would break down the mental faculties. In no mind does this principle become utterly extinct. Even the socially blighted misanthrope who flies from human society to the solitude of the wilderness or of mountain caves, and from that solitude imprecates curses upon the race, would find his mental desolation doubly desolate, were he informed that the race he curses had become extinct. Nor will he, in his exclusion from his kind, remain utterly alone; but will there encircle himself with his pet brutes. There is almost no form of good that we can fully enjoy without society of some sort. Society indeed gives value to all we possess. What we know would be painful to us, could we have no interchange of thought with

other minds, and our most delicious food would become loath-
some in the continued absence of all social endearments.

THE LOVE OF KINDRED.

The term *kindred* represents all relations by birth; such, for
example, as the parental, filial, and fraternal. In the condition
and well being of individuals within the circle of recognized
consanguinity we naturally feel, a deeper interest than we can
entertain towards individuals of the same class not thus related
to *us,* and this interest is generally proportionate to the nearness
or remoteness of the relation referred to. The most endearing of
all, is that which exists between the parent and the child, and
next to this in strength is the tie that binds together those who
derive their being from a common parentage. The affection of
the parent for the child is generally deeper than that of the child
for the parent. By some also maternal affection is regarded as
more intense than paternal. But which is the strongest and most
enduring, it would be difficult to determine. The absolute universality of the form of affection under consideration undeniably evinces, that it has its cause in an original principle of
human nature, and not in the mere external relations of the
parties concerned. Such relations, add to the strength of the
affection; but cannot account for its existence in the form in
which it appears among mankind in all conditions of society.
When these affections exist in their purity, and are attended
with a cordial fulfillment of the duties arising from the varied
relations of the parties concerned, they impart an ineffable
beauty and attractiveness to character. When they become
causes of blind partiality in respect to their objects, or obstacles
to the stern discipline of duty, then they impart to character its
most unattractive aspects, and become fruitful causes of
individual and social demoralization. Of all forms of worldly
endearment, none are so tender and happifying as those induced
by the domestic affections, when they exist in their purity, and
when love, in all its manifestations, conforms to the law of
duty. On the other hand, no forms of hate can be so embittered
and enduring as that which obtains when discord disturbs the

peace and harmony of the domestic circle; this law of the sensibility holding universally, that in those relations where the most beautiful harmony and the most blissful endearments should obtain, the wildest disorder, and most embittered malignity may be induced.

LOVE OF THE SEXES.

The love which, from the original principles of our nature, exists between the sexes, takes on two forms;—that of general interest, and that which constitutes the basis of the marriage union. Individuals of each sex are naturally more interested in those of the other, than of their own. The natural desire for the respect of individuals of the other sex,—a desire which dwells in the minds of men and women in common, is one of the chief regulative principles in respect to good manners and good morals in society. When members of either sex, to the exclusion of individuals of the other, are massed together for any considerable time, they naturally become vulgarized in manners, and degenerate, in morals. A properly regulated intercourse of the sexes, on the other hand, in families, in schools, and in society generally, tends, unconsciously to all to be sure, to the development of the most genial manners and the most perfect morals, which communities can possess. In the intercourse of society, and that on account of original and necessary tendencies of our nature, forms of exclusive affection are generated between individuals of opposite sexes, forms of affection which induce the mutual desire for the most intimate and enduring union known among mankind, a union never to be dissolved but by the death of one of the parties. The affection that lays the basis for this union has this peculiarity about it, that when, by the mutual vows of the parties in marriage, it takes on the form of duty, it becomes absolutely permanent in its existence and activity, unless limited by crime on the part of one, or both of the parties concerned.

THE LOVE OF FRIENDS.

In our intercourse with our kind, we meet, from time to time, with individuals whose spirit possesses a special *geniality* for our own, and with whom, as a consequence, we delight to associate. Social intercourse, under such circumstances, induces a mutual attachment between such individuals and ourselves, an attachment of a peculiar and special kind, represented by the term *friendship.* This conscious mutual geniality is the exclusive condition of friendship. When this is felt, as the result of social intercourse, this relationship is established, and when it is not felt, that relationship never exists. Various characteristics of men and women, may command our admiration, or esteem. Nothing, however, but this sentiment of mutual geniality induces that form of endearing attachment, known as friendship. Individuals may have many admirers, and even attached disciples, but no real friends. Individuals, on the other hand, with no qualities which command special admiration or esteem, may have many friends. There are individuals of high and commanding characteristics, who pass through life with little or no experience of true friendship. The reason is obvious. They have no social geniality of temperament which draws other minds into endearing intercommunion with their own. When the geniality under consideration obtains, all forms of real excellence combine with this, to strengthen and perpetuate the bonds of friendship. The real condition of friendship, however, is not, as already stated, any special forms of excellence, intellectual or moral. Even in heaven, where all are morally perfect, special genialities may induce special intimacies known even there by the name of friendship; and among the lost for aught we know, forms of geniality may obtain among individuals on account of which they may be known as friends.

Friendship induces universally special confidences, and one immutable condition of the perpetuity of this tenderly endearing relation is, that confidence shall, in no case, be betrayed; for confidence betrayed sunders the bond forever.

As natural affection may be supplanted by feelings of the bitterest malignity, the same holds true of the ties of friendship. There are few individuals towards whom we can experience feelings of deeper repulsion than towards those whom we have once known as special friends, the ties that once united us to them having been rudely sundered. Misanthropy is the almost exclusive result of affection blighted by cruelty, confidence rudely betrayed, and friendship repulsively broken. This principle almost, if not quite universally prevails in regard to the affections now under consideration. When once changed to indifference, coldness, or aversion, the tenderness which formerly obtained is never again renewed. As friendship is one of the sources of the purest bliss ever known, so its loss leaves a pang in the breast which hardly any cause can soothe, and time can hardly remove. If you have gained a real friend, think yourself happy indeed. If you have lost such a friend, regard the loss as a great calamity. The love of society, of kindred, of the sexes, and of friends, all in common, and each in particular, have their origin in distinct and original principles of our sensitive nature. From the immutable principles of that nature, we not only desire society, but as naturally seek, in society, for intercommunion with genial minds whom we can recognize as friends.

THE LOVE OF HOME.

"Home, home, sweet, sweet home!
There is no place like home."

What is it that renders that sentiment so genial to all minds in common? It is an original principle of our nature, which generated the universal desire to have some one spot, which, in all our wanderings, we may regard as our special dwelling place,—the place to which we hope to return as out permanent abode. This spot is represented by the term *home,* and the affection which consecrates it, and renders it sacred in our esteem, is the *love of home.* As we naturally desire the perfection of all objects which we love, so we as naturally desire to beautify home with every conceivable charm. The love of home is one of the great civilizers of society.

201

THE LOVE OF COUNTRY, OR PATRIOTISM.

Why did Mr. Peabody send his munificent gifts across the ocean, to enrich the institutions, and educate the poor of his native country, instead of devoting the same to the institutions and poor of other nations? and why does the world commend the direction which he has given to the mass of his benefactions? We account for both these facts, by referring to a fundamental principle of universal human nature, patriotism, or the love of country. The proper exercise of this affection does not involve hatred of other nations, or indifference to the rights or interests of any human being. It does imply what should exist in all minds, a form of special love for the land of our birth. This is natural to man in all conditions of existence. The affection of which we are now speaking, in its varied manifestations, takes on the form of zeal for the perfection of the government, administration, laws, and institutions of one's country, and for whatever tends to its highest prosperity, together with a jealous regard for its honor. In its perverted form, it harmonizes with the base maxim, "Our country, right or wrong."

LOVE OF THE SPECIES.

By an original principle of our nature, we are impelled to will the good of all men, without distinction of race or color. Under the influence of this affection, we naturally participate in the joys and sorrows of our kind, rejoice in their prosperity, and regret their adversities; we reprobate injustice and oppression, and rejoice in the triumph of justice, truth, and liberty among all nations, and in all communities, in common. Whenever and wherever, a human being lifts his manacled hands before us, and asks the question, "Am I not a man, and a brother" we do violence, not only to our intellectual and moral, but to original laws of our sensitive nature, when we turn from the suppliant, as if he was not a man, and our brother. We best obey the laws of our intellectual, spiritual, moral, and sensitive nature, when we make the sentiment of universal and impartial philanthropy our chief frame of mind. Of all the principles of our emotive and sensitive nature, activity under this one is least likely to lead us astray from the principles of truth and duty.

LOVE OF BENEFACTORS.

Years ago a Scottish nobleman died. At his funeral, a stranger to all present,—a stranger clad in deep mourning, appeared and took his seat with the mourners, and during all the services in the House of God, and at the grave, no one manifested deeper grief. At the close of the solemnities, he disappeared, and no one present ever saw or heard of him again. Among the papers of the deceased, a record to this effect was discovered. Whilst passing alone, and on horse-back, during a cloudy night, through a mountain gorge, he was stopped by a highwayman. The deep breathing and hesitation of the robber convinced the nobleman that it was the first crime of the stranger, and that he had been driven to the act by some very pressing necessity. On expressing his apprehensions, the nobleman was assured that he was correct. "What amount of money would bring you relief?" asked the nobleman. The sum was named, and the stranger was assured, that if he would appear at a certain place, the next day and give a sign then designated, the money would be handed to him, no questions being asked, and the recipient not being recognized. The amount pledged was handed over as promised. Just one year from that day, the gift, principal and interest, was, from a source unknown, remitted. So on every succeeding anniversary of that event, the same identical sum was always remitted. No one doubted that the recipient of the great relief, was the stranger mourner referred to. This was, and is, gratitude, an affection which always implies a *cherished remembrance of the gift received,* the most *kindly recollection of the giver,* and a *strong desire* to make full, and more thankful *returns* for the good conferred. "It is more blessed to *give,* than to *receive;"* yet few forms of joy lie deeper than those which attend the exercise of genuine gratitude. The benevolent affections, manifested in appropriate acts, impart an ineffable beauty to character. Gratitude cherished and duly manifested impart to character forms of beauty and perfection hardly less attractive. A coldly selfish mind is a blot and blank in the creation of God. An ungrateful recipient of kindly benefactions, is one of the most repulsive and odious objects that ever has place in the sphere of thought.

LOVE OF GOD.

By nature we are religious beings, and naturally delight in the contemplation of whatever is beautiful, grand, sublime, excellent, or perfect. The idea of infinity and perfection is the highest idea that can have a place within the sphere of thought. The idea of an eternal mind possessed of every possible mental attribute, and each attribute absolutely infinite and perfect, is the highest form which the idea of infinity can conceive. To this one idea, all the higher departments of our sensitive nature, the moral and spiritual, are immutably correlated. God must be to the mind the great, central object of thought and contemplation; and the consciousness of His approbation and favor ever must be the all-overshadowing want of its nature. Love to God, as a sentiment of our emotive nature, assumes the form of delight, wonder, awe, reverence, veneration, and adoration; as different attributes of the divine mind, and different relations of the infinite to the finite, become objects of thought and contemplation. When the mind is consciously pure in heart, "God is its everlasting light, and the days of its mourning are ended." When consciously impure, He can be to it nothing but an object of dread and terror. We close our elucidation of the affections with a few suggestions of a general nature in respect to them.

GENERAL CHARACTERISTICS OF THE AFFECTIONS.

1. They must each be referred, to distinct and original principles of our sensitive nature. Neither class can be resolved into one of the others; nor can they all be resolved into any one common principle.

2. The proper exercise of the affections is genial to our nature, and is attended with passive impressions happifying to the mind. They occasion pain when they take on the form of sympathy for the suffering; but even then they are universally agreeable.

3. The affections are, in themselves, disinterested. The well being of their respective objects, is regarded by the mind as a good in itself, irrespective of any reflex influence upon our own happiness.

4. In themselves, as mere impulsions of our sensitive nature, the affections have no moral character. They prompt to actions right or wrong, and under their influence, we may become virtuous or vicious. As mere states of the sensibility, however, they constitute us neither morally good nor bad.

5. As the affections must exist, excepting when extinguished, or turned to hate by crime in the subject, to be "without natural affection" implies moral depravity and criminality in their most aggravated forms.

6. The existence of the affections, resulting as they do from the original constitution of our nature, most strikingly evinces and illustrates the divine beneficence. God has so constituted us, that we are not only prompted to duty by conscience, but impelled to its performance by the original principles of our sensitive nature.

7. As the highest happiness results, when duty is discharged by all within the circle of the affections, so almost no form of unhappiness is more intense than that which results from duty violated within that circle. What a ceaseless gloom, for example, is thrown over an entire domestic circle, when one of its members falls into crime, or under the influence of some debasing vice. Just in proportion to the nearness of the relations existing between individuals, is their mutual power to render each other immeasurably happy or miserable.

CHAPTER VI.

THE DESIRES.

Our desires," says Mr. Stewart, "are distinguishable from our appetites by the following circumstances: 1st. They do not take their rise from the body. 2nd. They do not operate periodically after certain intervals, nor do they cease after the attainment of their object," a characteristic which desires possess in common with the affections. Sensations and emotions are passive states of the sensibility. Appetites, affections, and desires are active, or impulsive states of the same department of our nature. Appetites take their rise in the body, and tend towards physical gratifications. The affections impel us to seek the good of sentient existence around us. Those phenomena of the sensibility which impel the mind to or from varied objects of thought as distinguished from those of the affections, are denominated *desires.* Among these we shall consider the following:

The desire of continued existence,—The desire of action,—The desire of knowledge, or the love of truth,—The desire of esteem, objective and subjective,—The desire of power,—The desire of authority,—The desire or principle of imitation,—The desire of superiority,—The desire of hoarding,—and The desire or love of order.

THE DESIRE OF CONTINUED EXISTENCE.

When the mind attains to a distinct and reflective consciousness of the fact of its existence, it experiences an instinctive desire for the continuance of that existence. In the presence of the idea of the cessation of its physical being an irrepressible desire equally instinctive arises for a continuance of its mental being and activity in another state. Hence the hope of immortality "springs eternal in the human breast." This desire of continued existence is seldom repressed by the experience of unhappiness, and the extinction of hope. Even

206

the suicide cries: "Whence this secret dread, and inward horror of falling into naught?" This universal and instinctive desire for continued existence, "this pleasing hope, this fond desire, this longing after immortality," is an absolute pledge from the Author of our being, that mind will never cease to be.

THE DESIRE FOR ACTION.

"Weary of rest" is a poetic form of speech which represents another mental principle of our sensitive nature. Action, mental and physical, is one of the immutable demands of that nature. Thought, motion, activity, are essential elements of the true and proper life of mind; and when no specific forms of action seem demanded, we bestir ourselves to escape the weariness of inaction. The rest of heaven is not the rest of utter inaction, but forms of blissful activity that never tire. As opposed to a state of inaction, glorified spirits "rest not day nor night." As we are now constituted, action long continued, or violent, overtaxes our powers, and induces the pains of fatigue. Inaction is thus desired, not as a good in itself but as an alleviation. As soon as the powers become invigorated, however, action is desired as a good in itself.

THE DESIRE, OR LOVE OF KNOWLEDGE.

"For the mind to be without knowledge is not good." Universal human nature responds to the truth of that maxim. So strong is the desire for knowledge in the mind, that it often flies from ignorance, when assured, that "knowledge leads to woe." "Who would lose, though full of pain, this intellectual being?" This love of knowledge, as it exists in the mind, assumes two forms, a desire for a knowledge of facts, or mere information, and for science properly so called, that is knowledge in systematic form.

THE DESIRE OF ESTEEM.

The desire to know that we are possessed of the approbation and favor of others, minds, and to be conscious to ourselves, that we deserve the esteem which we enjoy, are the results of original and immutable principles of our sensitive nature. Desire in the form first named, is called the love of reputation, and in the second, self-esteem. Esteem in both forms is a good to universal mind, and within proper limits may be lawfully sought as such. As a mere impulse, however, it may prompt to good or bad actions and cannot, without crime, be indulged, to the sacrifice of moral principle in any form. To sacrifice reputation in order, by adherence to moral principle, to enjoy the conscious desert of the good sacrificed, is one of the purest and noblest forms of virtue.

DESIRE OF POWER.

A little child, in a state of the intensest and most ecstatic excitement, rushed to a neighbor who had called at its father's house, to announce the great fact, that it was then able to put on its shoes without the aid of others. What induced that fullness of joy in that child's mind? It was the consciousness of *power,* to which it had just attained. A similar love of power dwells in all minds. We love to exercise power over all objects around us, whether material or mental. Those spheres of activity which impart the most distinct consciousness of the possession and exercise of this one prerogative, are of all others preferred. When individuals become distinctly conscious of the possession of any particular kind of power, especially of the ability to exercise such power in its *perfected* forms, they experience a special delight in its exercise. When, for example individuals acquire real excellence of power in any department of thought or action, they will ever after find special pleasure in such forms of activity.

Here we have revealed an immutable principle which should govern the student, the apprentice, and the clerk, in all stages of their education. It is this: Aim to acquire the entire and conscious *mastery* of all that you attempt to learn. You will then not only possess real excellence in your future sphere of thought and action, but you will ever after find *real pleasure* therein.

THE DESIRE OR LOVE OF AUTHORITY.

At first thought, it would appear, that the love of authority is only a special form in which the love of power develops and manifests itself. Whether this, in fact is so or not, the former is so peculiar in itself, that it demands special notice. The relation of ruler and subject does not imply either mental or physical superiority in the former over the latter. The ruler of a kingdom, the president of this nation, or the governor of a state, is not always the wisest, nor the strongest individual in his nation or state. Yet the will of such ruler is, in many respects, *law* to his subjects, and this is what is meant by *authority.* We are so constituted by our Maker, that the exercise of such prerogative is a source of real delight and gratification. In the proper exercise of such prerogatives, the ruler is ennobled in public estimation, while the subject is not debased. To each of these relations, those of ruler and subject, our nature is fundamentally adapted. The people naturally delight in subjection to wholesome authority, while rulers are blessed in its exercise.

THE DESIRE OR PRINCIPLE OF IMITATION.

Man, in fundamental particulars, is, from the immutable laws of his being, a copyist. The child copies the man, and as imitative beings, our speech, our manners, and to a great extent, our morals, unconsciously take form from those of the community around us. We naturally dislike to be singular, and he is a moral hero who dares to do right, in opposition to general example around him. The power which *fashion* sways over community has its basis in the principle under consideration. Other influences combine with this to give it power, such for example, as the love of country, reverence of ancestry, respect for associates, and the principle of friendship. The power of *example,* also, has its chief foundation in the principle under consideration. What others do, we are naturally inclined to copy. Hence any form of activity which constantly stands revealed before us in living example, we almost unconsciously take on.

THE LOVE OF SUPERIORITY.

When we witness any form of activity performed by others, we are naturally inclined, not only to repeat the same, but as naturally desire to *excel* what we perceive to have been done. The desire to excel does not imply delight in the want of excellence in others; nor that theirs shall be less than ours actually is. On the other hand, when we know what others are, or can do, we naturally desire to reach a higher degree of excellence, and rejoice in the thought that we have greater forms and degrees of excellence than they possess. That such is the constitution of our nature is undeniable, and to it the progress of society towards higher and higher forms and degrees of excellence is chiefly owing. Nor is action under this principle wrong in itself. My neighbor for example, does well in some given department of thought or activity in which I am engaged. Where is the wrong in my desiring and aiming to attain to a form of excellence more perfect than his? If this desire induces, in me the spirit of envy, jealousy, or detraction, here is a moral wrong, and that wrong consists, not in the mere desire entertained, nor in any form of proper action under it, but in violating, under the influence of that desire, the law of duty.

THE DESIRE OF HOARDING.

Whatever is to us an object of interest and delight, we naturally desire to possess, and to retain for future use and enjoyment when possessed. The idea, that any form of good is ours, that we have an exclusive right in it, and control over it, is to our minds a source of great delight, and enjoyment. The same feeling naturally induces the desire to gain possession of such forms of good which are not now under our control. Thus we have the desire of property, or the love of hoarding,—a universal principle of human nature.

THE DESIRE OR LOVE OF ORDER.

"Order is heaven's first law," as a consequence, the *love of order* is a first and fundamental attribute of universal mind. There is a natural and universal desire for knowledge systematized, for facts classified under general principles, and that all things be conformed to rules of order. The absence of order, in any department of thought or action, is to the mind a source of deep disquietude. Order is the immutable condition of efficiency in every important sphere of thought and action.

GENERAL REMARKS UPON THE DESIRES.

A few remarks of a general nature are required upon the subject before us.

1. The phenomena included under each of these classes, are to be referred to distinct and original susceptibilities of our nature, for the obvious reason that neither can be resolved, into any or all of the others; nor into any other principle of our nature. Yet they appear as universal and positive impulses of the sensibility.

2. Each of these principles is disinterested in this sense, that the object is sought for its own sake, as a good in itself, and not on account of any consequences near or remote, anticipated from, nor under any more general impulse of our nature, such as self-love. We do not, for example, first say, that knowledge will make us happy, and then seek it for that reason. Before any such reflex calculations were made, knowledge was regarded as a good in itself, and on its own account; and as such it was desired. So of each of the other classes referred to.

3. Our desires are *impulsive,* not *regulative* principles of action. Each desire impels the mind towards its own, and away from every other, object. The intelligence must determine which is to be gratified on any particular occasion, and how far.

4. These principles of our nature present a striking illustration of the divine beneficence. Whenever we are pursuing any object, with any reference to our general well being, we are always gratifying some one or more definite demands of our nature. The farmer, when laboring to provide for the maintenance of himself and family, is not obeying merely the impulse of conscience, self-love, and paternal affection. Many other

principles of his nature combine their influence to render labor itself a good.

5. I will here notice a mistake into which, as it appears to me, many philosophers have fallen in regard to the active principles now under consideration. We are so constituted, it is said, that the value of present attainments, is always lost with the attainment itself, while the mind is borne on after new objects. Thus man, from the constitution of his being, is under the influence of perpetual delusions, seeking as a good, that which experience perpetually affirms to be "vanity and vexation of spirit." This is true, only when inferior objects are sought, not as a good, but as the ultimate, the supreme good. Then human nature is to itself a perpetual lie, and then only.

6. The mistake of many Christians in endeavoring to destroy their own, or the hold of sinners upon the world, by descanting upon the vanity of worldly pursuits, is obvious. They thus represent nature as a lie, and God as requiring gratitude for that which is not a good.

The desires which we have been considering, may be called primary. We have others which may be called secondary, or artificial. That which conduces to gratify natural desire, will be desired as means to that end. So when we have willed the attainment of any object, a law of our nature impels us to desire and seek it. A large portion of our desires are of this class.

CHAPTER VII.

GENERAL ACTIVE PRINCIPLES.

Among the general active principles of universal mind, the following require special attention; to wit, the principles of self-defense, self-love, conscience, and the love of justice.

SELF-DEFENSE.

That this principle is a universal law, not only of rational, but also of irrational, sentient existence, is obvious to the slightest observer of the facts which surround us. I may also remark that there are few individuals, who, under certain circumstances, would not yield to the impulse of this law. My object on the present occasion is, not so much to inquire into the lawfulness of self-defense, nor if lawful, when and by what means, but to inquire into the nature of the feelings which arise under such circumstances. The causes which excite these feelings are the action of certain powers which endanger, either our lives or our particular interests. The causes may be intelligent or unintelligent. In either case the first feeling excited is the emotion of fear or apprehension. Hence a desire arises to escape the impending evil,—a desire impelling us either to remove ourselves from the presence of the cause, or to arrest or destroy the action of the cause itself. In case the cause is an intelligent one, the desire is associated with feelings of displeasure towards the agent himself, strongly impelling us to prevent the evil intended, by destroying his power to inflict it. On this feeling I deem it important to make the following remarks:

1. As an original impulse of our nature, it has no moral qualities.

2. It differs in kind from revenge. To ward off a blow aimed at my body, or simply to disarm the individual who aims the blow, and then to proceed to inflict positive injury upon him after he is disarmed, are totally different things.

3. This is a universal principle operating in regard to all interests, real and assumed, right or wrong.

4. It is under the cover of this principle, that almost all injuries inflicted upon men are perpetrated.

5. Virtue, and moral excellence can never be hated by us except when they are placed before the mind; as opposed to the inflexible purposes of our will, or to some darling gratification upon which our hearts are set.

6. An inquiry purely ethical demands a passing remark here: Within what limits may we lawfully yield to the impulse under consideration? Just so far, I answer, as to prevent the occurrence of the impending evil. Whatever injury the antagonist must endure in order to accomplish this, can never be laid to our account.

SELF-LOVE.

This is a feeling or impulse of our nature,—an impulse connected with the idea of well-being; an idea elucidated in a former chapter, and shown to be a necessary conception of the reason. The term well-being should be understood as applicable to our entire existence. The feeling under consideration, impels the mind to sacrifice present pleasure, when necessary to secure our general well-being, and to endure present evils for the same reasons. I remark:

1. This impulse differs in kind from all the other impulses, such as appetites, desires, and affections, which were illustrated in former chapters. These are all particular, and impel the mind towards present gratification, irrespective of the future. Hence it often happens, that the impulses arising from the action of these propensities, coincide with, or are opposed to the impulse under consideration. The determinations of the will are accordingly sometimes in conformity with one, and sometimes with the other.

2. Equally distinct is this principle from selfishness. The former simply impels the will to choose our own happiness. The latter consists in yielding to this impulse when our interests are opposed to the higher good of others.

3. This is a rational active principle, the impulse being conditioned on the development of the idea of well-being.

4. The mistake of utilitarians in maintaining that this is the only active principle of our nature now becomes obvious. Self-love, as we have seen, is totally distinct from all our particular propensities, and but for their influence, as President Wayland has shown, would exist in the mere form of desire, impelling to no particular acts whatever. It is only one among many other active principles of our nature.

CONSCIENCE.

The ideas of right and wrong, of merit and demerit, based upon the two former; and of reward and punishment based upon those of merit and demerit, and conscience considered as the testifying state of the reason, have been sufficiently illustrated in former chapters. It only remains here to analyze the phenomena of the sensibility connected with the above ideas. To accomplish this, I remark:

1. That in all right and virtuous actions there is perceived by the mind a certain intrinsic beauty, fitness, and propriety, which perception is attended with those delightful emotions which the idea of beauty, and of moral beauty alone can excite. Precisely the opposite feelings are awakened by the contemplation of what is wrong.

2. In reference to the above perceptions there is always a strong feeling of love or hate, impelling us to choose the one and reject the other. That is what is called the impulsive power of conscience.

3. When we have done right or wrong, there is always a judgment that we deserve reward or punishment, and also a judgment or expectation, that we shall receive the due reward of our deeds. These judgments are always attended with certain feelings of delight and joyful anticipation, or of anguish and fear, which are called the testimony or joys of a good conscience, or the pangs of remorse.

Now that function of the reason which gives us the judgments above referred to, together with the functions of the sensibility, which give existence to these feelings, constitute those complex operations of the mind, denominated conscience. Conscience is neither the former nor the latter, considered by themselves, but both together. Hence conscience has been wrongly defined, as a mere susceptibility, on the one hand, and as an exclusively rational faculty, on the other.

LOVE OF JUSTICE.

In the presence of actions right or wrong, all men not only judge that the agents deserve reward or punishment, but experience what are called feelings of good-will, or the opposite, —feelings or desires, impelling us to choose, that the virtuous may be happy, and the vicious miserable. This is a universal and necessary impulse of our nature, and constitutes what is called the love of justice or of moral order. This principle, in case of aggravated guilt, induces the will to turn inward, and prey upon the mind itself. This is the last stage of human anguish.

CHAPTER VIII.

COMPLEX PHENOMENA.

We come now to our second general inquiry in regard to the phenomena of the sensibility,—an inquiry which respects those states of mind which have generally been regarded as simple feelings, but which, in reality, are complex states, composed of certain feelings associated with the action of the intelligence or will, or both.

In approaching this subject I would first direct attention to a few fundamental principles connected with the inquiry before us, and upon which all our subsequent conclusions will be based.

1. The spontaneous and necessary phenomena of the sensibility and intelligence, are alike destitute of all moral qualities.

2. We are accountable for *voluntary* states of mind only, i. e. for those states the existence and perpetuity of which depend, either directly or indirectly upon our will.

3. In respect to all complex states of mind, which are characterized as right and wrong, the moral and voluntary elements are always identical, the other elements being right or wrong, not in themselves, but because their existence depends upon the other or voluntary element.

Hence, we clearly perceive,

4. The error of certain philosophers and divines who place all that is right or wrong in moral agents, in right or wrong *feelings;* whereas feelings, in themselves, are neither right nor wrong. Also,

5. The error of those who attempt, from the above proposition, by appealing to complex phenomena of the mind as if they were simple states, to prove, that feelings, in themselves, as mere spontaneities of the sensibility, are possessed of a moral character.

Attention is now invited to a consideration of some of the complex phenomena of the mind above referred to.

WISHING.

That we do often regard such states of mind as possessing of a moral character is a matter of universal consciousness. Desiring and wishing are often, in common parlance, used synonymously, and as such, a moral character is often and with propriety attributed to each. But desire properly speaking, as shown in a former chapter, is simply an impulsive state of the sensibility, in reference to certain objects, a state necessarily and in itself destitute of all moral qualities. A *wish* on the other-hand, is a desire perpetuated, by a concurrence of the will with the desire. Now when this desire is thus perpetuated and directed towards a required or forbidden object, this complex state of mind designated by the phrase, I wish, assumes a positive moral character.

LUSTING.

Lusting considered simply as a state of the mind, irrespective of external actions, is the concurrence of the will with the impulse of desire, when directed towards a forbidden object. The external act is only this choice of the will acted out. The guilt of the act rests in the previous wish or choice.

COVETOUSNESS.

This is a concurrence of the will with the impulse of desire, when directed towards that which belongs to another. As such it is the parent of crime, and consequently its prohibition is numbered among the fundamental prohibitions of the divine law.

HOLINESS—VIRTUE AND VICE.

At this place I deem it important to point out the nature of holiness and sin, virtue and vice, and those characteristics by which one is distinguished from the other. Holiness and virtue, which are in reality but different names for the same thing, consist in the subjection of the will to the dictates of conscience,—in other words, to the divine will, so that all our other powers and principles are subjected to this one principle.

Sin and vice, on the other hand, consist in the subjection of the will to other impulses of our nature in opposition to conscience or the will of God. A sinner is a creature of mere impulse. The strongest feeling, for the time being, controls him. A holy or virtuous being is one who subjects all the impulses of his nature to the will of God, as apprehended by the conscience. All the forms of virtue are expressed in the Bible by the word *love*. The opposite word, on the other hand, expresses all the forms of vice or sin, to wit, *selfishness*. Of the nature of love, as above presented, we will inquire in subsequent chapters. Attention is now invited to a few general remarks upon the nature of

SELFISHNESS.

Selfishness as very generally understood, consists in a supreme regard for our own happiness. To say in this sense that all men unrenewed by the grace of God, are supremely selfish, is contradicted, for example, by all the instances of parental affection which may be seen throughout the world. But the selfishness of such persons, in the sense of the word above explained, will readily appear when the strong action of parental affection is met by some principle of duty, in the ready subjection of the latter to the former. In this sense, all unrenewed men are supremely selfish. They regard their own gratification above all other considerations. In whatever direction the stronger impulse of the sensibility directs them, thither they go, regardless of right, regardless of their own, or of the general well being of others. We have already considered two forms of selfishness; to wit, lusting and coveting. Attention is now invited to a third.

HATRED, WRATH, MALICE.

In a former chapter we have seen, that whenever another individual is contemplated as exerting his power in opposition to our purposes or interests, a strong feeling of displeasure, called anger, necessarily arises in our minds, a feeling impelling us to prevent the injury by destroying his power to inflict it. Now this feeling will be temporary or permanent, just as the opposition in question is regarded as permanent or temporary. When the will coincides with this impulse and thus perpetuates its existence, the complex state of mind thus induced is called hatred. When directed towards personal objects it is the hatred forbidden in the Bible. Wrath and malice are hatred, in its more excited forms; the former in what maybe called the more tempestuous, the latter in the more deliberate form.

GLUTTONY.

This has been commonly defined to be excess in the use of food. Considered as a state of mind, it is the subjection of the will to the impulse of appetite, and that in opposition not only to the dictates of conscience but also of self-love.

LICENTIOUSNESS.

Considered in the form of lust, consists in the unrestrained license to sin, and in the unlimited concurrence of the will with this impulse, whatever its direction may be. In reference to such persons, nothing but the absence of the impulse, and of the possibility of indulgence, will prevent the commission of adultery or fornication. "Their eyes are full of adultery, and cannot cease from sin."

AVARICE.

Consists in the subjection of the will to the love of hoarding in reference to money; or to those objects for which money is commonly exchanged.

REVENGE.

Revenge is sometimes used to designate the operation of the principle of justice, the operation in which deserved retribution upon criminals is not only wished, but sought. As such it is attributed to God, and instead of being wrong, it is to be numbered among the brightest virtues. But revenge, as prohibited in the Bible; consists in that kind of concurrence of the will with the spirit of anger, wrath, and hatred, in their forbidden forms, which were described above,—a concurrence in which a gratification of this spirit is sought by inflicting upon an individual or individuals an injury corresponding to an injury, real or supposed, received from them. I receive a blow or an injury from some individual. Instead of suppressing the feeling of displeasure thus excited, I yield to its influence by seeking to inflict a corresponding injury upon the offender. This is revenge. The ways in which the infliction of the injury may be sought, are various; as, directly through our own instrumentality, or by imprecating the interposition of divine power, or by endeavoring to associate the influence of others with our own, against the object of our displeasure. In the last sense, revenge most commonly assumes the form of slander, detraction, defamation, and evil surmisings, evil speaking, etc.

PRIDE.

Pride and humility are defined by Dr. Brown, as "those vivid feelings of joy and sadness, which attend the contemplation of ourselves when we regard our superiority or inferiority, in any qualities of mind or body, or in the external circumstances in which we may be placed." Again: "When I define pride to be that emotion, which attends the contemplation of our excellence, I must be understood as limiting the phrase to the *single emotion that* immediately follows the contemplation." If this is pride, it is certainly a very innocent feeling and we may well wonder that such heavy denunciations are made against it in the Bible. The command also, "Let the brother of low degree rejoice in that he is exalted," must be considered as a direct command to be proud. Lost spirits also, we must infer, will be very humble at the resurrection; for it is declared that they shall be filled with shame in view of their conscious degradation, the very essence of humility, as defined by the above named author. No wonder also, that this writer represents pride not as "excusable merely, but praiseworthy."

Pride, as defined by others, consists in *inordinate* self-esteem. If so, I reply it is a mere blunder, a misjudgment. Further, the consequent or the effect, has, in the above definition, evidently been mistaken for the cause. The misjudgment is evidently caused by pride pre-existing in the mind.

What then is pride? I answer: It, is the subjection of the will to the control of the desire of esteem, or the love of power, or both united. Its very essence consists in choosing, or willing as the supreme good, our own exaltation. "Thou shalt be as gods." Choosing this as the great good, is *pride,* and as such is the essence and cause of almost all sin. When this end is thus chosen, the subject may very easily assume that he is what he really desires to be, and hence pride and inordinate self-esteem are very commonly united. But this is by no means the case universally. Pride is often attended with conscious degradation, and thus as we say is mortified. When an individual judges himself to have obtained the elevation desired, and the judgment is based upon the possession of things great in themselves, such as wealth, knowledge, or power, this judgment is attended with a feeling of joyful exaltation, which, with the concurrence of the will with the feeling in question, induces the individual to assume those lofty airs denominated haughtiness. When the judgment in question is based upon the possession of trifling excellences, such as a superior equipage, a beautiful face, or a graceful form, the concurrence of the will with the feeling thus excited, constitutes what is called vanity. Again: When an individual under the influence of pride, perceives in the possession of others that which he desires as the means of self-exaltation, or when the possessions of such individuals are regarded as a barrier to the attainment of the desired object, the concurrence of the will and the feeling of regret and hatred thus excited constitute *envy.*

Envy in its turn, becomes the fruitful cause of heart burnings, detraction, slander, and evil speakings, and a host of other nameless crimes, of which pride, is the root and fountain.

EMULATION.

When other individuals are seen to possess that which secures to them the esteem desired, pride induces its subjects to seek a superiority in respect to the same possessions, as a means to the end desired or willed. In this form pride assumes the aspect of emulation.

AMBITION.

Ambition is only one form of pride, and differs from emulation only in respect to its objects. It consists in willing not only a superiority to others as a means of self-exaltation, but everything else which may be regarded as a means to that end. Ambition, when its control becomes supreme, is perfectly reckless of means. All things are lawful which contribute to the end in view. As such it is not only incompatible with the existence of virtuous principles, but of virtuous action, when the individual becomes subject to strong temptation. No principle is so dangerous in the education of the young as an appeal to ambition, and the spirit of emulation in the pupil. As far as the pupil yields to the influence brought to bear upon him, the formation, not merely of a religious, but in the common acceptation of the term, of a virtuous character, becomes an absolute impossibility.

JEALOUSY.

Jealousy is the twin sister of envy. As envy induces the subject to take from others that which, in our possession, will exalt us or, if possessed by others, will prevent our exaltation, jealousy leads one individual to suspect in others the same designs which he is cherishing towards them. To the envious mind all beings are enemies, either as possessing that which makes him wretched, or as designing to take from him that which he values above all price.

CHAPTER IX.

RELIGIOUS PROPENSITIES.

In treating upon this subject, I shall notice the various religious affections in the order in which, as a general fact, they are developed in Christian experience, and in which they are presented in the Bible. I shall make no apology for departing from the common course in making an analysis of the religious affections a part of a system of mental philosophy. That they have not constituted a part of such courses shows, either that those who have most profoundly studied mind, have very commonly disregarded its moral laws, or at least, that religion has not had that place in philosophy which its importance demands.

Before entering particularly upon a consideration of the peculiar characteristics of any of the religious affections, I will give a brief recapitulation of some of the topics illustrated in the preceding chapters as preparatory to their full and distinct elucidation.

Every phenomenon of human consciousness, as we have seen, belongs either to the intelligence, the sensibility, or the will. The phenomena of the first two, bear the characteristics of necessity, those of the latter, that of liberty in opposition to necessity. In the will, and in the will only, is man a subject of moral government,—a free accountable agent. In respect to none of the phenomena of the sensibility, or of the intelligence is he accountable, only so far as their existence and character depend upon the will. Here we are presented with the great problem in theology: In what sense is man accountable for his feelings and the convictions or judgments of his intellect? In other words, in what sense do they depend upon the will?

In regard to such an inquiry we may remark in general, that when we are brought into such relations to truth in any form, that honest integrity on our part, will induce a knowledge and belief of said truth, then ignorance and disbelief are both criminal. So when any feelings tending to moral wrong are voluntarily entertained, so that they take on the form of wishing relatively to their objects, then our criminality is the same in kind as when the prohibited act is performed. When any feelings prompt to moral wrong, and these are promptly suppressed and held in subjection, there is, not criminality, but moral virtue.

Into all the religious affections, I remark, in the next place, each one of the mental faculties, the intellect, sensibility, and will, enters and exercises its proper functions. These functions will be designated in the following elucidation. The religious affections will also be treated as simple states of consciousness, without reference to their *origin* or *cause.* Whether they are, like other states, the pure results of truth, or whether they are the results of a supernatural, divine agency, pertains to the science of Biblical theology, and not to mental science. Having made these remarks we commence our elucidation with the subject of

REPENTANCE.

In every mind, there is an immutable conviction of actual violations of the law of duty, that is of sin. A benighted heathen, when asked the question, "Are you not a sinner?" Replied: "Do you suppose that I am such a fool as not to know that?" The sentiment expressed by the words, "I am a sinner," constitutes the common conviction of the race. Here is the part which the intellect takes in this exercise. While this conviction exists in the mind, as it universally does, it may be voluntarily entertained, with a view of all the consequences it involves, and all the duties it imposes; or it may be resisted, and as far as may be, neglected or suppressed. The mind may, also, voluntarily entertain the conviction, that for sin it has no excuse; it may sincerely confess, condemn and reprobate its inexcusable criminality and ill-desert, and as sincerely abandon all forms of wrong doing, and yield up all its powers with the full and sincere intent to conform to all the demands of the law of duty in all future time; or it may assume the attitude of self-justification, hide, instead of confess, its criminality, and hold on in the way of transgression. Here we are presented with the voluntary elements which characterize *impenitence,* on the one hand, and real repentance, on the other. In the latter state, there is, first of all, a voluntary entertainment and admission of the *fact* and inexcusableness of personal sinfulness, with all the consequences and duties which that fact involves,—voluntarily confessing, condemning, and reprobating this fact, and that before and to all concerned, the mind then abandons and rejects sin in all its forms, and with sincere "purpose of heart," adopts the law of duty as the immutable rule of its future activity. This, I repeat, is repentance, contemplated as a voluntary mental state. These convictions, purposes, and acts, are attended, of necessity, with certain emotive states, feelings of deep sorrow, regret, hatred of wrong, and desires for entire moral purity and obedience to the will of God and the law of duty,—emotive states denominated in the Scriptures "godly sorrow," on the one hand, and "hungering and thirsting after righteousness," on the other. Such is that complex mental state represented by the word, repentance.

FAITH.

In universal mind, these convictions, among others, have a prominent place,—that God is infinite and we are finite,—that God is independent and that we sustain to him the relations of absolute and universal dependence,—that God is merciful and we are sinners,—that God, as our creator and preserver, is our lawgiver and judge, and that we as his creatures, are bound to make his will the absolute law of all our activity;—that while our necessities are infinite, there is in God a perfect and available fullness to meet them all, and that relatively to all our real interests, God, to meet them, is absolutely trustworthy. When the mind distinctly and voluntarily recognizes the validity of these convictions, and by a sealing act of moral election, intrusts its mortal and immortal interests to the divine care and keeping, accepting and trusting the will of God as the law of its activity, it then puts forth that mental exercise denominated faith,—faith the fundamental element of which is trust,—confidence voluntarily reposed in ascertained trustworthiness. Faith in God is trusting him universally and absolutely, and obeying him implicitly under the conviction of his universal and absolute trustworthiness. Faith is not trusting, in the absence of valid reasons, but confidence reposed in the presence of valid reasons for its exercise. In other words, faith in God is absolute respect for absolute trustworthiness. Unbelief, on the other hand, is the absence of this respect; it is disbelief, or voluntary dissent, entertained and cherished in the presence of reasons of infinite weight for assent; it is respect withheld from known trustworthiness.

The view of faith above given obviously corresponds with the teachings of inspiration upon the subject. In the Old Testament, it is represented by such words and phrases as "staying the mind on God," "trusting in him," "placing our hope and confidence in God," and "committing our spirits to His hands," all implying, as its fundamental characteristic, *trust* voluntarily exercised towards God, on the ground of his known trustworthiness.

A few words may be necessary to explain the nature of that form of faith which respects Christ, as its special and specific object. The revealed mission of Christ is to save lost men from their sins. Faith in him in this relation has its basis in the conviction of personal sinfulness, on the one hand, and of the absolute *trustworthiness* of Christ, to save from their sins all who put their trust in him for such salvation on the other; and consists, in its essential nature, in trust voluntarily reposed in him for this one end, *salvation from sin.* This act of trust is also attended with a voluntary surrender of all our powers and interests to his control. This is what is meant by the words, *believing in Christ,* as they are employed in the New Testament. So the apostle Paul expressly teaches. "I know," he says, "whom I have believed, and am persuaded that he is able (trustworthy) to keep that which I have committed (voluntarily intrusted) unto him against that day."

The emotive states attending the exercise of faith always correspond to the nature of the truth apprehended, and the attitude in which it is contemplated at the moment, emotive states represented by such terms and phrases as "quietness and assurance," peace with God, "joy in God," "joy unspeakable and full of glory."

Into the exercise of faith every power and susceptibility of the mind enters and bears its appropriate part. Some truth is apprehended by the intellect. The effect upon the sensibility, or the feelings excited are in accordance with the nature of the object of contemplation, while the determinations of the will correspond with the feelings of the heart and the convictions of the intelligence.

LOVE.

To bring this subject distinctly before the mind, it may be well to cite a few passages of Scripture in which it is contained. For example: "On these two commandments hang all the law and the prophets," "Love is the fulfilling of the law." "All the law is fulfilled in one word, love."

From these, and other passages of a similar nature, we learn, that love constitutes the essential element of every state of mind that is morally virtuous. The precept requiring love embraces every precept of the moral law, and constitutes the only element which renders obedience to that law virtuous.

Our first inquiry is, What is the fundamental element of love,—that element particularly and primarily referred to in the command requiring it?

That form of love which is the fulfilling of the law cannot, of course, be found in any mere convictions of the intelligence. These, fallen spirits possess in common with the pure and holy. Nor can it be found in any mere *emotive* states. If such states did possess, in themselves, moral character, which, as we have seen, is not a fact, they do not, undeniably include *all* duty to God and man, which they would, if *all* the law is fulfilled in them.

That form of love in which "all the law is fulfilled," is *attended* with corresponding intellectual and emotive states, but is not found in these. Where then, shall we find it? In voluntary states exclusively. When all voluntary states and exercises of the mind fully accord with the requirements of the law of duty, in all their forms,—duty to God, to man, and all sentient existences, then the whole law is fulfilled. In the Scriptures, love and obedience are affirmed to be identical. "He," says Christ, "that hath my commandments, and *keepeth* them, he it is that loveth me." "This," we are told, "*is* the love of God, that we *keep* his commandments." *Doing* righteousness, we are also told, constitutes us righteous beings. When the will, is rightly adjusted towards God and all sentient existences who have claims upon us, then we have fulfilled the law. The Scriptures, science, and the intuitive convictions of the race, unite in affirming the validity of this view of the subject. An important inquiry here arises; to wit, what are the feelings by which those acts of the will called love are accompanied? To this question, the following general answer may be given. The emotions accompanying the exercise of love will always correspond to the nature of the beloved object, and the particular attitude in which it is contemplated.

1. The object may be contemplated as possessed of high moral excellence. It is then chosen as an object of endearing contemplation, association, and imitation. The consequent effect upon the sensibility will be the excitement of intense emotions of attachment and delight.

2. This excellence may be contemplated as associated with high natural and intellectual characteristics; such as, wisdom, knowledge, and power. There is then in the exercise of love, a voluntary surrender of ourselves to the control of a being superior to ourselves; while the feelings excited are those of esteem, veneration, awe, and adoration.

3. The beloved object may be contemplated as regarding us with approbation and favor, or as sustaining to us the relation of a benefactor. We then experience emotions of high gratification and delight, and the feeling denominated gratitude.

4. We may contemplate the object loved as being honored or dishonored by others. Feelings of intense delight and gratification are experienced in the former case, and of regret, indignation, and zeal for his injured honor in the other.

5. We may contemplate ourselves as having offended the object of our affection. Love then assumes the aspect of sorrow, penitence, and contrition.

6. The object under consideration may be contemplated as in a state of suffering and affection. Love then assumes the attitude of sympathy or pity.

7. Finally, we may contemplate the object beloved as guilty of crime. We then desire, and consequently will, his return to virtue, which state of mind is accompanied with feelings of deep and intense sorrow and regret.

The effect of a consciousness of the exercise of this virtue will be internal peace, and confidence in the approbation and favor of all virtuous beings.

CHRISTIAN WARFARE AND VICTORY, AND SELF-DENIAL.

In the varied circumstances of life, events occur, and conditions of existence arise, in which our emotive and sensitive states induce desires impelling the will in the direction of prohibited gratifications. When all such impulsions are resisted, subdued, and held in subjection to the will of God and the behests of conscience, then that form of Christian virtue is exercised, denominated *patience.* The mental conflict with evil principles within, and temptations to wrong from without, which attend the exercise of this virtue, is called the *Christians warfare,* or "the fight of faith," while its conquest over the propensities to evil is denominated, "the *victory that overcomes the world."* The act of obedience by which all the propensities are held in subjection to the will of God, and the law of duty, by which present gratifications strongly desired are refused, present sacrifices are voluntarily made and present evils are endured, to secure the higher ends of benevolence, and maintain subjection to the behests of conscience, is called *Christian self-denial.*

HUMILITY.

Among the most prominent of all the varied forms of Christian virtue, is that represented by the term *humility,* a term commonly employed to represent that lowliness of mind, deep sense of personal unworthiness, self abasement, penitence, quietude of spirit, and submission to the divine will, which always attend genuine conversion. This virtue does not consist, as some appear to suppose, in entertaining the sentiment that we are greater sinners than others; that we possess, as Christians, no real virtues, or that we are really worse than we actually are. While the Scriptures, and reason too, prohibit our forming too high an estimate of ourselves,—"thinking of ourselves more highly than we ought to think," they do absolutely require that we form just and true estimates of our real and relative merits and demerits, excellences and defects; in short, that we know ourselves as we *are,* and not as we are not, that we "think *soberly, according* as God hath dealt to every man the measure of faith." When the mind attains to this real self-knowledge, humility consists in a full and cordial assent on its part, to be known and esteemed by the Judge of all, by ourselves, and all intelligences, in perfect accordance with its real and *relative* deserts; and that all others, those superior to ourselves especially, shall occupy similar positions in universal regard.

THE FILIAL SPIRIT.

In the Scriptures we are taught, that it is an immutable condition of admission to the kingdom of heaven, that men "be converted, and become as little children." Much is said also of the spirit of *adoption,* the filial spirit, with which all that are truly "born of God," become imbued. What is this spirit? What are its essential characteristics?

Inspiration, I remark in reply, reveals Jehovah, not only as the Creator, Preserver, Governor, and Judge of all, but as sustaining the most intimate and endearing *parental* relations to all the pure in heart. He is revealed as their Father, and Friend, "their shield and exceeding great reward," as entertaining the tenderest sympathy with them in all their joys and sorrows, pleasures and pains, cares and perplexities, as being ever present with them as their teacher and guide, and the affectionate guardian of all their interests, and as a propitious hearer of prayer, opening upon their minds, by his own Spirit, visions of his glory and love, and bringing them into direct fellowship and intercommunion "with the Father and with his son Jesus Christ."

Now when the fatherhood of God in all the endearing relations above referred to, is distinctly recognized by the mind, when the exercise of the varied forms of trust, confidence, prayer, fellowship, and intercommunion with God, become habitual in its experience; and when it, as habitually "casts all its cares upon Him," with the deep assurance that in all our afflictions He is afflicted;" when the promised divine teaching and illumination are sought and enjoyed, and every indication of the divine will is cordially met and acquiesced in, then the mind is in the exercise of the spirit of adoption, the filial spirit, under consideration. When, on the other hand, the habitual dwelling place of the mind is under the shadow of the sterner attributes of God,—his justice, unapproachable purity, all-searching scrutiny, and eternal judge-ship, then it is subject to "the spirit of fear which gendereth to bondage." When, finally, *all* the divine perfections, in their true relations, the mild and the stern, the sweetly attractive and awe inspiring, are habitually before the mind, then it naturally exercises the filial affection and confidence, on the one hand, and the "Godly fear," on the other, which constitute the highest possible perfection of Christian character.

The *emotive states* which attend the exercise of the filial spirit of Christianity, are such as these; deep delight and joy in God, assurance of hope, universal satisfaction with providence, filial gratitude for favors received, and quiet acquiescence when they are withheld, and when, afflictions cast their shadows over the mind; all together constituting a repose of spirit, and fullness of blessedness, which make the nearest possible approach to "the rest that remains for the people of God."

A SPIRIT OF FORGIVENESS.

When an injury is forgiven, the offender is treated with the same kindness as if he had never offended us. Here we find the fundamental element of love, which for the interest taken in the well-being of another, consents to treat the offender as innocent. The condition required of the offender, is repentance. Without this, forgiveness, properly speaking, is an impossibility, or if possible, a sin. The case of an offender who continues incorrigible, comes under another duty which we shall shortly consider.

FORBEARANCE.

This consists in holding back from the offender the execution of deserved vengeance for the purpose of bringing into that state in which he can be forgiven. Its language towards the offender is this: With your present character, it is impossible for me to regard and consequently treat you as a virtuous man. My desire however is, that by repentance, humility, and forgiveness sought, you may show such a regard to rectitude that I may treat you as virtuous; when this is done, you will be to me as if no offense had ever been received. Such is the forbearance of God. "The goodness, (or forbearance) of God leadeth thee to repentance."

CONDESCENSION.

This virtue is benevolence or love exercised towards persons occupying stations beneath us, and consists in descending to a level with them; and, in this sense conforming ourselves to their capacities, cultivating their friendship and their society for the purpose of elevating them in the scale of being and worth to a level with ourselves. It stands opposed to pride in this sense: pride places itself upon the apex of the pyramid, choosing that others, whatever their worth may be, may occupy places at a respectful distance below. Condescension descends to the base, for the purpose of helping others up to the wide prospects we ourselves enjoy. The following truths present this virtue to the mind of the Christian, as a duty and privilege.

1. The essential equality of men.

2. Hence the desire that they may possess those privileges, the want of which in their case, and the possession of which in ours, has made the difference between them and ourselves.

3. The fact that we are what we are in consequence of the infinite condescension of God.

4. The universal example of God.

MEEKNESS.

Has reference to the manner in which forbearance, condescension, etc., are exercised; to the kind, mellow, and gentle spirit with which injuries are endured, and the repentance of the offender sought and a "soft answer" returned to his abuses.

THE STERNER CHRISTIAN AFFECTIONS.

Christian character is a reflex of "the image and glory of God,"—the finite receiving and reflecting the infinite; hence this form of character, like its divine original, has in it the mild and the stern, the tender and the severe; mercy and justice, delight in goodness and reprobation of evil, all blended in harmonious unity. Individuals who suppose, that Christian character in its perfected forms, is made up of that kind of good nature which contemplates with an equally immovable complacency the just and the vile, truth and falsehood, the oppressor and the oppressed, are fundamentally mistaken. The throne of God and the Lamb, is encircled with the mild radiance of the bow of peace and promise. Within the circle of that bow, however, "there are thunderings, and voices, and earthquakes, and great hail." While God is revealed as "merciful, and gracious, long suffering, and slow to anger," he is also revealed as "angry with the wicked every day." Christian character, in its perfected forms, is in full correspondence with its divine original.

PART III.

———

THE WILL.

The will has already been defined, as that faculty of the mind to which all mental *determinations* are to be referred,— determinations such as *intentions, purposes, resolutions, volitions,* and *choices.* No additional considerations need be presented to prove, that this faculty stands at an equal remove from the intelligence, on the one hand, and the sensibility, on the other. No philosopher of any distinction *now* questions the threefold division of the mental faculties, adopted in this treatise. While the will is to be regarded, as a *separate,* it is, by no means, to be considered as an *independent,* faculty. All its acts of every kind, are put forth in view of some object or end apprehended by the intelligence, and in connection with some movement of the sensibility. Each of these faculties, also, is influenced by the action of each of the others. Each, however, has its own peculiar sphere, and in that sphere, is governed by laws equally special and peculiar.

POINTS OF AGREEMENT AND DISAGREEMENT AMONG PHILOSOPHERS.

There are certain questions in the department of mental science, in which all philosophers of any note now agree. They generally agree, as stated above, in the validity of the threefold division of the mental faculties presented in this treatise, the intellect, sensibility, and will. They also perfectly harmonize in the doctrine, that the two faculties first named, are, in fact, governed, in all their activities, by one fixed and immutable law, that of *necessity*. They differ, some of them fundamentally, in regard to the question, whether the will is also subject to this law, or to that of *liberty* as opposed to *necessity*. This is one of the leading issues in the sphere of mental science. What I now propose to do, is to enable the inquirer after truth to settle this issue satisfactorily to himself.

THE TERMS LIBERTY AND NECESSITY DEFINED.

To accomplish this object, we must, first of all, most clearly and specifically define the two apposite ideas represented by the terms liberty and necessity, when they stand opposed, the one to the other. The term liberty is sometimes used in opposition to the term servitude. The idea which it then represents is wholly diverse from that which it represents when it stands opposed to the term necessity. What are the distinct and opposite ideas represented by these terms, when they stand opposed the one to the other?

These terms, I answer, when thus opposed to each other, represent two distinct and opposite relations which may be supposed to exist between a given *antecedent* and its con-*sequent*. The first relation is this: the antecedent being given, but one consequent can arise, and that must arise. This is the exclusive relation represented by the term, necessity. The second relation referred to is this: the antecedent being given, and in connection with the same identical antecedent, either of two or more consequences may arise, and neither, in distinction from the other must arise. It is self-evident, that every antecedent and its consequent must fall under one or the other of these relations. All acts of will are, as we have seen, preceded by certain intellectual, and sensitive, and emotive states, tending to influence its determinations. These states (motives) are the antecedents to said acts, and the acts are the consequents. All such acts,—the consequents,—must sustain to the states or motives referred to,—the antecedents,—the relation of liberty or necessity, as these terms have been above defined. If a given act is free or necessary, it is, and must be, absolutely so.

A FREE AND NECESSARY AGENT DEFINED.

Man, then, is a *free* agent, if, in the identical circumstances in which he does put forth given acts of will, he *might* put forth *different* and opposite acts from those which he does put forth. He is a *necessary* agent, if in the identical circumstances in which he does put forth given acts of choice, he could *not* put forth different and opposite ones. The same holds absolutely true of all other agents, and this is the fixed and immutable definition of a free agent, on the one hand, and of a necessary agent, on the other. So far, then, as free agency is to be affirmed of any being, necessary agency is to be absolutely *denied* of him, and vice versa. Is man, then, a free or necessary agent?

HOW THIS QUESTION MUST BE ANSWERED.

There are but two sources of ultimate appeal in answering such a question,—the affirmations of our own interior consciousness,—and the testimony of the author of mind, testimony given in his own word; and these sources of appeal originating as they do from the same infallible author, must be in harmony, as far as they relate to the same facts. In a former part of this treatise, we have seen, that in all positive mental states, we have an absolute consciousness, not only of the states themselves, but also of ourselves, as the subjects of them. Now if, in this state of consciousness, we do, or do not, have absolute knowledge of the actual relations of ourselves to the states referred to, we either can, or cannot, by any appeal to consciousness, determine the question, whether we are free, or necessary agents. If, also, the Scriptures, by express teaching, or undeniable implication, do or do not affirm one or the other of these hypotheses, in opposition to the other, to be true, then we either can or cannot, by such an appeal, determine where the truth lies. If both these sources of appeal, should affirm the truth of either, and deny that of the other, then, we have absolute *proof* of the one thus affirmed. Let us now turn our thoughts to each source of proof in succession, and see if we can, or cannot, find the truth after which we are inquiring.

TESTIMONY OF CONSCIOUSNESS.

Let us suppose ourselves in the presence of some object of choice, an object in respect to which one of two or more distinct and opposite determinations must be put forth. What is the state of our consciousness in regard to these diverse determinations? But one answer can, in truth, be given to this question. We are just as conscious of absolute power to put forth either, in distinction from the other, as we are that we exist at all. When we put forth one determination, we do it with the *absolute consciousness* that we might, in the same circumstances, have put forth either of the others. When in subsequent times, we remember that act of choice, that remembrance is always accompanied with the consciousness equally absolute, that we might have put forth different acts of choice from what we did originate. This absolute consciousness of absolute free agency accompanies all our acts of choice. The conclusion is undeniable. We are free, and not necessary, agents, or the universal consciousness is an *absolute lie.* Whatever our *theory* in regard to the doctrine of the will may be, this is the absolute testimony upon the subject which we all receive in the interior of our own consciousness. To deny the validity of the testimony which we here receive, is, in fact, to impeach the integrity of the Author of the power of consciousness itself.

We all have the consciousness, also, that we are not only *free,* but *moral* agents. When the right and the wrong are before us, as objects of choice, we recognize our obligations as absolute to choose the one, and eschew the other. When the act of choice has been put forth, we approve or condemn the act, and affirm ourselves as deserving of good or ill, in absolute accordance with the relations of our acts of choice to the law of duty.

Upon one immutable condition can we affirm our personal responsibility for acts of choice; to wit, that we are in fact *free* and not necessary agents. An individual, we will suppose is, *by no fault of his,* but by the will of Providence, placed in circumstances in which none but a prohibited act of choice is possible to him, and that act he *must* put forth. We can no more conceive him to be blameworthy for any such act, than we can conceive of the annihilation of space; and God himself, has thus constituted our intelligence. The immutable characteristic of all so called wrong acts, rests upon the supposition, that we are free agents. God himself, in the fundamental laws and constitution of the universal consciousness and general intelligence, has thus made Himself responsible for the validity of the doctrine of the free agency of man.

EVIDENCE FROM INSPIRATION.

The Scriptures give us no direct and immediate revelations pertaining to the science of mind. Man stands therein revealed, and known as the subject of *moral government,* and by consequence, as possessed of all the powers of moral agency. He is everywhere addressed by commands and prohibitions, requiring him, under sanctions of infinite weight, to reject the evil and choose the good. For wrong doing under all circumstances, he is affirmed to be wholly without excuse.

All such teachings undeniably imply in man absolute free agency, the power, when he does right or wrong to choose the opposite. On no other conditions is it even conceivable, as we have seen, that he should be responsible for his acts of choice. God, we will suppose, and this is just what he does do, if the doctrine of necessity is true, God we will suppose, places a creature in circumstances in which he cannot but sin, that is, choose the wrong. Is it conceivable, that he should be blameworthy for doing that which it is impossible, and God has rendered it impossible, for him not to do? Upon one condition exclusively, and that from the nature of universal mind, as God himself has constituted it, can the judgments of the Most High stand revealed to the eye of the rational creation, "as true and righteous altogether;" namely, that good and evil are equally, and at all times, and under all circumstances, *possible* to all whom God treats as moral agents.

God does, in fact, let me add, place creatures, and that without their choice, in circumstances in which they *do* sin. He then expresses the deepest regret, and even wonder and astonishment, and calls upon heaven and earth to be astonished with him at the fact, that, under those identical circumstances, they do sin. If the doctrine of necessity is true, God entertains the deepest regret, and calls upon the universe to unite with him in wonder and astonishment, that that should occur the non-occurrence of which he himself has rendered absolutely impossible. Man, then, is a free, and not a necessary agent, or the human intelligence is a lie, and inspiration, a mass of contradictions and absurdities.

OBJECTIONS.

Against the doctrine above elucidated, many and grave objections may be urged, and have been urged, objections lying within the sphere of theology, on the one hand, and of philosophy, on the other. These objections, however, are all comprehended under the following forms.

THE DIVINE FOREKNOWLEDGE.

It is a revealed fact, it is urged, in the first place, that our acts of choice are foreknown to God, a fact which could not be real, were the will free, and not subject to the law of necessity. This objection, I reply, rests upon the assumption that the divine foreknowledge is based upon the same conditions that ours is. *We* can foreknow none but necessary events. How do we know, that the divine foreknowledge is subject to the same limitations? As an absolutely conscious, and also, as a revealed, fact we *know* that we are, not necessary, but free, agents. On the authority of inspiration, we *believe,* that our free acts are foreknown to God. These two facts we hold as real, because we have valid evidence for thus holding them. Their compatibility with each other, we do not profess to explain, for the all-adequate reason, that we do not understand the conditions, limitations, or *quo modo,* of the divine foreknowledge.

THE WILL AS THE STRONGEST MOTIVE.

It is further urged against the doctrine of free will, that all our acts of choice are in fixed accordance with the *strongest motive,* which would not be the case, were we free, and not necessary, agents. When the objector is asked to fix definitely the meaning which he attaches to the words, strongest motive, his invariable reply is this; that is the strongest motive which the will does, in fact, follow: Let the argument on which this objection rests, be put in a logical form, and its absurdity will become self-evident. It then stands thus. If the will always follows the motive which it does follow, it is subject to the law of necessity; it does, in fact, invariably follow the motive which it does follow; therefore, it is, in all its acts, subject to this one law. Whether God has, or has not, "left free the human will," this truth still remains, that this faculty, in all its acts, does follow some motive, and that motive is the one which it does follow.

If the words, *strongest motive,* be defined, as they should be, to mean the strongest *desire,* or what the intelligence affirms to be *best,* it will then stand revealed, as an absolute truth, that in neither of these senses, is the will always as the strongest motive. In acts of moral wrong, the will follows the strongest *feeling* in opposition to the dictates of the intelligence. In doing right it not unfrequently holds in *subjection* the strongest feeling, while it yields obedience to the behests of conscience.

WE ARE CONSCIOUS OF CHOOSING, BUT NOT OF LIBERTY IN CHOOSING.

In reply to the appeal made to consciousness in favor of the doctrine of free will, it is affirmed, that we are conscious of our acts of choice, as mere facts, and not at all of the power of free choice. This objection, I remark, is based wholly upon a total misinterpretation of the knowledge which is derived from consciousness. In respect to all mental states in common, we are, as we have seen, not only conscious of the same as facts, but of ourselves as subjects of, and of our relations to, said states. In our intellectual and sensitive states, we are not only conscious of the same, but of ourselves in them, as subject to the law of necessity. In all acts of choice, we are not only conscious of said acts, but of ourselves in them as exercising the responsible functions of free, in opposition to necessary, agency. No other exposition correctly interprets real knowledge by consciousness.

RELATIONS OF THE WILL TO MOTIVES.

All acts of will, as has been before shown, are put forth in view of motives of some kind. In the absence of all motives, it is self-evident, that no such acts of any kind are possible. In one respect pertaining to this subject, there is now coming to be a general agreement among philosophers; to wit, that while the motive is the *occasion*, it is not the *cause proper* of acts of will. In the presence of motive, the question what specific act shall be put forth does not depend upon the *motive,* but upon the *power of free choice* in the will itself.

In one respect, however, the motive is the cause proper of acts of will. In the presence of a given motive, the will *must* act in *some* direction. So far motives sustain to such acts the relations of real causes. In the presence of motives for the right and the wrong, for example, the will is not free to do the one or the other, or not to act at all. It *must* do the right, *or* the wrong. So far, it is not free at all. In respect to the question, *which* it shall do, here its freedom is absolute. The same holds true, in respect to all motives of every kind.

UNIVERSAL PRINCIPLE IN REGARD TO THE LIBERTY OF THE WILL.

In regard to the will, this principle with strict universality obtains. So far forth as its activity is free *at all,* so far is its power of free choice absolute; and so far it, or any other power, is subject to the law of necessity, it is, in no sense, free.

INTENTIONS, CHOICES, VOLITIONS, PREFERENCES, ETC.

Acts of will are classed, as *intentions, choices, volitions,* etc. Intentions are those controlling acts to which others are subordinate. Choices are those acts in which a selection is made between different objects presented to the mind's election. Preferences are acts of choice which accord with the strongest desire. Volitions are executive acts by which intentions are, or are attempted to be, realized. A man's intention, we will suppose, is to take a journey. All those subordinate executive acts by which that intention is sought to be carried out are called volitions.

In intentions and choices we are, and in preferences and volitions we are not, free. In the two former, we are conscious of absolute freedom. By definition, we cannot put forth an act of preference but when choice accords with the strongest feeling. Volitions being subordinate executive acts, must from the nature of the case, be as the intentions to which they are subordinate, and the former being given, the latter must be.

Intentions take rank, as subordinate, and ultimate. The former are those controlling acts to which volitions of a certain class are, or may be, subordinate. The latter are those acts of will to which intentions and volitions of certain classes may be subordinate, but which are themselves subordinate to no other acts. The term motive is sometimes employed as synonymous with intention.

As intentions control all other acts of will, the moral character of the latter always is as that of the former. This statement accords with teachings, not only of inspiration, but with those of philosophers and theologians universally, as well as with the intuitive convictions of the race.

POINTS OF GENERAL AGREEMENT IN RESPECT TO
THE DOCTRINE OF THE WILL.

In concluding this last department of our present inquiries, I would specify the points of agreement which have now generally obtained in the spheres of both philosophy and theology, in regard to the doctrine of the will. They are, among others, the following:

1. The validity of the doctrine of a tri-unity of the mental powers denominated the intellect, the sensibility, and the will.

2. That man is free, if free at all, only in respect to the action of the will.

3. That he is directly and immediately responsible but for acts of will, and that the moral characters of all such acts are as those of our ultimate intentions.

4. That for our other mental states: viz., those of the intelligence and sensibility, we are accountable so far forth only, as their existence and character depend upon the action of the will.

244

5. That in all complex mental states of which moral character can be predicated, the voluntary and moral elements are identical.

THE IDEA OF LIBERTY AS OPPOSED TO THAT OF SERVITUDE.

The term liberty sometimes represents, not only an idea opposed to that represented by the term, necessity, but one opposed to that represented by the term, servitude. In the latter sense, we are free when, and only when, all our voluntary activity is in harmony with the conscience and the law of duty, and all the impulsions of the propensities are held in strict subordination to the law of conscience and duty. We are in a state of moral servitude, when the propensities control the will in opposition to the behests of conscience and duty. The form of servitude thus resulting, and the degradation implied, depend upon the character of the controlling propensity, the lowest and most degrading of all being that in which the animal in man obtains the ascendency. The term liberty, or freedom is employed to designate the former state, because, that, in it, in the exercise of the high prerogative of self-control, the mind always does that which it approves and delights in. The latter state, on the other hand, is represented by the term servitude, because that, in a state of conscious enslavement to the lower propensities, it does that which it necessarily reprobates and abhors.

THE WILL AS SUBJECT TO THE LAW OF HABIT.

It is a fixed law of all the mental faculties in common, that action in any given form, generates a tendency to continued action in the same form, a tendency which is increased by each repetition of the same act. Under this law the will is constantly acting. In doing the right or the wrong, we are not only incurring the desert of praise or blame, but we are constantly forming fixed habits which tend to perpetuate action, in all future time, in the same direction. These habits,—for the formation of which we are responsible, at length become so fixed, that all prospect of change totally disappears.

THE CHARLES G. FINNEY PROJECT.
BY ALETHEA IN HEART MINISTRIES.
THE LIFE AND WORKS OF CHARLES G. FINNEY.

Volume

1. Lectures on Revivals of Religion, 1835, 1868.

2. Narrative of Revivals, or The Revival Memoirs of Charles G. Finney, 1869.

3. Skeletons of a Course of Theological Lectures, 1840.

4. *American* Lectures on Systematic Theology, 1846. Vol. I.

5. *American* Lectures on Systematic Theology, 1847. Vol. II.

6. Lectures on Systematic Theology, *Final* 1851 London edition. Vol. I.

7. Lectures on Systematic Theology, *Final* 1851 London edition. Vol. II.

8. The Character, Claims and Practical Workings of Freemasonry, 1869.

9-16. The Published Sermon Collection.

17. The Published Letters.

18. Life Work and Memories of C. G. Finney by his Associates, Students, and Friends.

19. Theological and Philosophical Lecture Notes.

20. Miscellaneous Letters, Sermon Outlines, Articles, and a Detailed Subject and Scriptural Index of the Complete Works.

Reproduction of the complete works with detailed indexes in hard and soft covers, to be available in print individually and in a complete series; on CD with full searching capabilities; also recorded on tapes, CDs, and DVDs.

Work books and multimedia helps to be created to assist in the private or classroom study of these volumes. A presentation of the influence of Finney upon the church and world to be given through the *American Reformation Project*.

www.ingramcontent.com/pod-product-compliance
Lightning Source LLC
Chambersburg PA
CBHW031505270326
41930CB00006B/253